NEW TESTAMENT READINGS & DEVOTIONALS

New Testament Readings & Devotionals

VOLUME 1

C.M.H. Koenig

Robert Hawker
Charles H. Spurgeon
Octavius Winslow

C.M.H. Koenig Books

C.M.H. Koenig Books
Copyright © 2021 by Heather L. Rautio

All rights reserved. No part of this book may be reproduced in any manner whatsoever without written permission except in the case of brief quotations embodied in critical articles and reviews.

ISBN 978-1-956475-24-1 (Paperback)
ISBN 978-1-956475-25-8 (eBook)
ISBN 978-1-956475-26-5 (Hardcover)

Scripture quotations, unless otherwise noted, are from the Christian Standard Bible. Copyright © 2017 by Holman Bible Publishers. Used by permission. Christian Standard Bible®, and CSB® are federally registered trademarks of Holman Bible Publishers, all rights reserved.

Scripture quotations marked AKJV are from the Authorized (King James) Version. Rights in the Authorized Version in the United Kingdom are vested in the Crown. Reproduced by permission of the Crown's patentee, Cambridge University Press.

Cover design by H. L. Rautio.
Cover photograph by W. M. Rautio.

First Printing, 2021
Second Printing, 2024

Visit www.cmhkoenigbooks.net

Contents

Preface   xi
Compiler's Note   xiii

1	Reading: Luke 1	1
2	Reading: John 1:1-14	4
3	Reading: Matthew 1	6
4	Reading: Luke 2:1-38	8
5	Reading: Matthew 2	10
6	Reading: Luke 2:39-52	12
7	Reading: Mark 1	14
8	Reading: Luke 3	16
9	Reading: Matthew 3	18
10	Reading: John 1:15-51	20
11	Reading: Matthew 4	22
12	Reading: Luke 4	24
13	Reading: Luke 5	26
14	Reading: John 2	28

15	Reading: John 3	30
16	Reading: John 4	32
17	Reading: Mark 2	34
18	Reading: John 5	36
19	Reading: Mark 3	38
20	Reading: Luke 6	40
21	Reading: Matthew 12:1-21	42
22	Reading: Matthew 5	44
23	Reading: Matthew 6	46
24	Reading: Matthew 7	48
25	Reading: Luke 7	50
26	Reading: Matthew 8:1-13	52
27	Reading: Matthew 11	54
28	Reading: Matthew 12:22-50	56
29	Reading: Luke 8	58
30	Reading: Matthew 13	60
31	Reading: Mark 4	63
32	Reading: Mark 5	66
33	Reading: Matthew 8:14-34	68
34	Reading: Matthew 9	71
35	Reading: Matthew 10	73
36	Reading: Mark 6	76
37	Reading: Luke 9:1-17	78

38	Reading: Matthew 14	79
39	Reading: John 6	81
40	Reading: Mark 7	83
41	Reading: Matthew 15	85
42	Reading: Mark 8	87
43	Reading: Luke 9:18-27	89
44	Reading: Matthew 16	92
45	Reading: Mark 9	94
46	Reading: Luke 9:28-62	96
47	Reading: Matthew 17	98
48	Reading: Matthew 18	100
49	Reading: John 7	104
50	Reading: John 8	106
51	Reading: John 9:1-10:21	108
52	Reading: John 10:22-42	110
53	Reading: Luke 10	113
54	Reading: Luke 11	115
55	Reading: Luke 12	117
56	Reading: Luke 13	119
57	Reading: Luke 14	121
58	Reading: Luke 15	123
59	Reading: Luke 16	125
60	Reading: John 11	127

61	Reading: Luke 17	130
62	Reading: Mark 10	133
63	Reading: Matthew 19	135
64	Reading: Matthew 20	137
65	Reading: Matthew 21	139
66	Reading: Luke 18-19	142
67	Reading: Mark 11	144
68	Reading: John 12	146
69	Reading: Mark 12	150
70	Reading: Matthew 22	152
71	Reading: Luke 20	154
72	Reading: Luke 21	156
73	Reading: Matthew 23	159
74	Reading: Mark 13	161
75	Reading: Matthew 24	163
76	Reading: Matthew 25	165
77	Reading: Mark 14	167
78	Reading: Matthew 26	169
79	Reading: John 13	171
80	Reading: Luke 22	173
81	Reading: John 14	175
82	Reading: John 15	178
83	Reading: John 16	180

84	Reading: John 17	182
85	Reading: Mark 15	185
86	Reading: Matthew 27	188
87	Reading: John 18	190
88	Reading: John 19	192
89	Reading: Luke 23	195
90	Reading: Mark 16	197
91	Reading: Matthew 28	199
92	Reading: John 20	202
93	Reading: John 21	204
94	Reading: Luke 24	207

Works Cited	209
About The Authors	210
C.M.H. Koenig Books	211

Preface

New Testament Readings & Devotionals, Volume 1 features the four Gospels: Matthew, Mark, Luke and John. The primary focus is the life, death, and resurrection of our Lord Jesus Christ.

Estimated Timeline: 5 BC – AD 33

About the series:

The readings and devotionals series compiled by C.M.H. Koenig consists of eleven (11) volumes for the Old Testament and three (3) volumes for the New Testament. They combine a chronological reading plan of the Bible with a related devotional for each "reading." Each reading is generally one chapter and the associated devotionals are excerpts from Robert Hawker (1753–1827), Charles H. Spurgeon (1834-1892), or Octavius Winslow's (1808-1878) works. The Psalms are interspersed throughout the Old Testament volumes.

The intent of the series is to help us savor the scriptures and, in the words of the Psalmist, to "Taste and see that the LORD is good" (Psalm 34:8, CSB).

Charles Spurgeon commended Robert Hawker with these words: "Gentleman, if you want something full of marrow and fatness, cheering to your own hearts by way of comment, and likely to help you in giving your hearers rich expositions, buy Dr. Hawker's Poor Man's Commentary. ... he sees Jesus, and that is a sacred gift, which is most precious whether the owner be a critic or no. There is always such a savor of the Lord Jesus Christ in Dr. Hawker that you cannot read him without profit."

Unless otherwise noted, the key verse(s) for each day (in italics) are from the Christian Standard Bible (CSB).

For more information, visit C.M.H. Koenig's website at: www.cmhkoenigbooks.net.

Compiler's Note

Spelling & Grammar:

Some of the spelling has been standardized with modern or American English spelling, such as "traveller" to "traveler," or "neighbour" to "neighbor." All references to "the Holy Ghost" have been standardized to "the Holy Spirit."

Since these writings were taken directly from the authors' original works, there may seem to be some grammatical errors by modern practice. By and large, the grammar remains unchanged from the original text in the cited works.

Scripture References:

The works in this compilation often refer to scripture other than the key verse(s) or scripture reading passage. Some are cited in the original works and others are not. Scripture reference citations contained in the original works as well as additional reference citations added by the compiler are listed at the end of each devotional, as needed, to facilitate cross-reference study. Scripture quoted within the devotionals are direct quotes or paraphrases from the Authorized (King James) Version of the Bible, unless otherwise noted in the original text.

1

Reading: Luke 1

"He has satisfied the hungry with good things and sent the rich away empty." Luke 1:53

Beware of placing any limit whatever to the grace of Jesus. Be your circumstances what they may; remember that "God is able to make all grace abound towards you; that you always, having all sufficiency in all things, may abound to every good work."[1] Make no allowance for sin, frame no excuses for inactivity, shrink from no cross, be disheartened by no difficulty, give place to no temptation, yield to no excessive grief; for Jesus has spoken it, and He now speaks it to you, "My grace is sufficient for you."[2] Since, then, the grace of Jesus is illimitable, take with you in your journeying to the one Source of supply a vessel of large capacity that you may receive abundantly. Remember that, as a believer in the Lord Jesus, "All things are for your sake, that the abundant grace might, through the thanksgiving of many, redound to the glory of God."[3] Let your life be a perpetual traveling to this grace. Do not be satisfied with what you have already received. Go, again and yet again, to this Divine Fountain, taking every corruption as it is developed, every sin as it is felt, every sorrow as it rises, to Jesus; remembering for your encouragement, that though you have received much, yet "He gives more grace,"[4] and is prepared to give you much more than you have yet received.

Rejoice that the emptiness of the vessel is no plea against the filling of the vessel. If the Spirit of God has made you "poor in spirit," has wrought in you a "hungering and thirsting for righteousness," betake yourself to the grace of Jesus.[5] The full vessel He needs not, nor does the full vessel want Him. He invites, He draws, and He receives none save the empty. He will have all the honor of our salvation. He will magnify His grace in the creature's nothingness. Your emptiness shall eternally glorify His fullness. With the example and the words before me of him who styled himself the 'chief of sinners,' I hesitate not to encourage the greatest sinner to come to Christ. "Who was before a blasphemer, and a persecutor, and injurious: but I obtained mercy... And the grace of our Lord was exceeding abundant with faith and love which are in Christ Jesus. This is a faithful saying, and worthy of all acceptation, that Christ Jesus came into the world to save sinners, of whom I am chief."[6] Truly might he exclaim, "By the grace of God I am what I am."[7] Beware then, I beseech you, of going to Christ for salvation in any other character than as an empty sinner. Had the vessels been brought other than empty, to receive the miraculous oil, they would have been refused, filled though they had been with ambrosia itself. Nothing should mingle with the oil. Nothing should shade the luster of the miracle. And so is it with the grace of Jesus. Brilliant genius, profound erudition, costly benevolence, and the purest ethics of natural religion, avail nothing in the matter of the soul's salvation. These are the ambrosia, of which the vessel must be emptied before it comes to Christ. It must all be laid aside as constituting a plea of acceptance. The only plea admissible with Christ is that without His grace you perish forever. "Lord, save, or I perish."[8] (Winslow, Evening Thoughts, p. Mar 28)

Footnotes:
1. 2 Corinthians 9:8.
2. 2 Corinthians 12:9.
3. 2 Corinthians 4:15.
4. James 4:6.
5. Matthew 5:3, 6.
6. 1 Timothy 1:13-15.
7. 1 Corinthians 15:10.
8. Matthew 8:25.

2

Reading: John 1:1-14

"*The only begotten of the Father, full of grace and truth.*" John 1:14

Believer, you can bear your testimony that Christ is *the only begotten of the Father*, as well as the first begotten from the dead. You can say, "He is divine to me, if he be human to all the world beside. He has done that for me which none but a God could do. He has subdued my stubborn will, melted a heart of adamant, opened gates of brass, and snapped bars of iron. He hath turned for me my mourning into laughter, and my desolation into joy; he hath led my captivity captive, and made my heart rejoice with joy unspeakable and full of glory. Let others think as they will of him, to me he must be the only begotten of the Father: blessed be his name. And he is *full of grace*. Ah! had he not been I should never have been saved. He drew me when I struggled to escape from his grace; and when at last I came all trembling like a condemned culprit to his mercy-seat he said, 'Thy sins which are many are all forgiven thee: be of good cheer.'[1] And he is *full of truth*. True have his promises been, not one has failed. I bear witness that never servant had such a master as I have; never brother such a kinsman as he has been to me; never spouse such a husband as Christ has been to my soul; never sinner a better Savior; never mourner a better comforter than Christ hath been to my spirit. I want none beside him. In life he is my life, and in death he shall be the death of death; in poverty Christ is my riches; in sickness he makes my bed; in darkness he is my star, and in brightness he is my sun; he is the manna of the camp in the wilderness, and he shall be the new corn of the host when they come to Canaan. Jesus is to me all grace and no wrath, all truth and no falsehood: and of truth and grace he is *full*, infinitely full. My soul, this night, bless with all thy might 'the only Begotten.'[2] (Spurgeon, p. Evening May 10)

Footnotes:
1. Matthew 9:2.
2. John 3:16.

3

Reading: Matthew 1

"*Thou shalt call his name Jesus.*" Matthew 1:21 (AKJV)

When a person is dear, everything connected with him becomes dear for his sake. Thus, so precious is the person of the Lord Jesus in the estimation of all true believers, that everything about him they consider to be inestimable beyond all price. "All thy garments smell of myrrh, and aloes, and cassia,"[1] said David, as if the very vestments of the Savior were so sweetened by his person that he could not but love them. Certain it is, that there is not a spot where that hallowed foot hath trodden – there is not a word which those blessed lips have uttered – nor a thought which his loving Word has revealed – which is not to us precious beyond all price. And this is true of the names of Christ – they are all sweet in the believer's ear. Whether he be called the Husband of the Church,[2] her Bridegroom,[3] her Friend;[4] whether he be styled the Lamb slain from the foundation of the world[5] – the King,[6] the Prophet, or the Priest[7] – every title of our Master – Shiloh, Emmanuel,[8] Wonderful, the Mighty Counsellor[9] – every name is like the honeycomb dropping with honey, and luscious are the drops that distil from it. But if there be one name sweeter than another in the believer's ear, it is the name of Jesus. Jesus! it is the name which moves the harps of heaven to melody. Jesus! the life of all our joys. If there be one name more charming, more precious than another, it is this name. It is woven into the very warp and woof of our psalmody. Many of our hymns begin with it, and scarcely any, that are good for anything, end without it. It is the sum total of all delights. It is the music with which the bells of heaven ring; a song in a word; an ocean for comprehension, although a drop for brevity; a matchless oratorio in two syllables; a gathering up of the hallelujahs of eternity in five letters.

> *"Jesus, I love thy charming name,*
> *'Tis music to mine ear."*
> (Spurgeon, p. Morning Feb 8)

Footnotes:
1. Psalm 45:8.
2. Ephesians 5:23.
3. Matthew 9:15.
4. John 15:15.
5. Revelation 13:8.
6. Revelation 17:14.
7. Hebrews 4:14.
8. Isaiah 7:14; Matthew 1:23.
9. Isaiah 9:6.

4

Reading: Luke 2:1-38

"All they that heard it wondered at those things." Luke 2:18 (AKJV)

We must not cease to wonder at the great marvels of our God. It would be very difficult to draw a line between holy wonder and *real worship*; for when the soul is overwhelmed with the majesty of God's glory, though it may not express itself in song, or even utter its voice with bowed head in humble prayer, yet it silently adores. Our incarnate God is to be worshipped as "the Wonderful."[1] That God should consider his fallen creature, man, and instead of sweeping him away with the besom of destruction, should himself undertake to be man's Redeemer, and to pay his ransom price, is, indeed marvelous! But to each believer redemption is most marvelous as he views it in relation to himself. It is a miracle of grace indeed, that Jesus should forsake the thrones and royalties above, to suffer ignominiously below *for you*. Let your soul lose itself in wonder, for wonder is in this way a very practical emotion. Holy wonder will lead you to *grateful worship* and *heartfelt thanksgiving*. It will cause within you *godly watchfulness*; you will be afraid to sin against such a love as this. Feeling the presence of the mighty God in the gift of his dear Son, you will put off your shoes from off your feet, because the place whereon you stand is holy ground. You will be moved at the same time to *glorious hope*. If Jesus has done such marvelous things on your behalf, you will feel that heaven itself is not too great for your expectation. Who can be astonished at anything, when he has once been astonished at the manger and the cross? What is there wonderful left after one has seen the Savior? Dear reader, it may be that from the quietness and solitariness of your life, you are scarcely able to imitate the shepherds of Bethlehem, who told what they had seen and heard, but you can, at least, fill up the circle of the worshippers before the throne, by wondering at what God has done. (Spurgeon, pp. Eve, Jan 26)

Footnote:
1. Isaiah 9:6.

5

Reading: Matthew 2

"... For we saw his star at its rising and have come to worship him." Matthew 2:2

Reader! let you and I ponder well the sweet and interesting record here given of the birth of Christ. If angels, who needed no redemption, praised God at his birth, with what holy rapture and joy ought our songs to go forth in thanksgivings for the same. Behold! with what unequalled humbleness the Son of God, as man, when he came and tabernacled in our flesh, manifested himself to the church. But behold! how God the Father honored his nativity, in not only sending wise men from the east to worship him, but in causing a star to point to the Savior. Was not this indeed sweetly fulfilling that blessed scripture; *the Gentiles shall come to thy light, and kings to the brightness of thy rising.*[1] But did the Lord God, in order that his blessed Son should be known, grant such a starry influence to the wise men; and will he withhold the light of his grace from the hearts of his people? Will he not reveal Christ in all his glory, and suitableness, and all sufficiency, that, like them, we may fall down and worship him, and present him more than gold, and frankincense, and myrrh, even those graces of his Holy Spirit which are his own?

And was it needful that the Lord of life and glory should go down into *Egypt*, that what the Prophet had said of calling God's dear Son out of Egypt might be fulfilled?[2] Surely then, Lord, it must be needful to call all thy sons from the Egypt of this world; for all by nature are in that house of bondage, before that an act of sovereign grace hath called them out. Was Jesus, the holy, harmless, undefiled Lord Jesus, here also, as in a thousand other instances, the forerunner and glorious Head of his redeemed? Oh for grace to follow the Lamb whithersoever he goeth!

But Oh! thou true and only real Nazarite of God! Precious Jesus, thou art indeed the Branch, the Plant of Renown, the Spiritual Joseph of thy people, whose branches run over the wall. Blessings be on the Head of Him, and on the Crown of the Head of Him that was the *Netzar*, the Separate, from thy brethren! Methinks I hear my Lord again say, as he did once in the days of his flesh: *for their sakes I sanctify myself!*[3] Ever precious, and dear name, Jesus Christ of Nazareth! Thou art thy church's *Nazarene!* (Hawker, Poor Man's New Testament Commentary: Matthew-John, pp. 20–21)

Footnotes:
1. Isaiah 60:3.
2. Matthew 2:15; Hosea 11:1.
3. John 17:19.

6

Reading: Luke 2:39-52

"... Then they began looking for him among their relatives and friends. When they did not find him, ..." Luke 2:44-45

May we not gather a lesson of sweet instruction from the anxious and fruitless search the parents made for Jesus in the days of his flesh? What kinsfolks and acquaintances shall we now search among for the Savior? My soul! how little of Jesus is to be found in this Christless generation! What parlor conversation makes mention of his name? Is it not plain and evident, from the general, nay, almost universal, silence observed in all companies concerning his name, and offices, and characters, and relations, that Christ is not there? Shall we seek him among the professors of the gospel? Who are they that honor Jesus? Not they who deny his Godhead; not they who deny the influences of his Holy Spirit; not they who set up their own righteousness as part, or the whole, of their justification before God. Jesus is not in that house, in that family, in that heart, among that people who live in sensuality, profaneness, and impiety. Where shall we seek Jesus? Blessed Lord! mine eyes are unto thee to be taught. I would say unto thee, in the language of the church,

"Tell me, O thou whom my soul loveth, where thou feedest, where thou makest thy flock to rest at noon. O, when I shall find thee without, I would lead thee, and bring thee into my mother's house, who would instruct me; and I would cause thee to drink of spiced wine of the juice of my pomegranate."[1] (Hawker, The Poor Man's Morning Portion, p. 178)

Footnote:
1. Song of Songs / Solomon 1:7; 8:1-3.

7

Reading: Mark 1

"Immediately they left their nets and followed him." Mark 1:18

When they heard the call of Jesus, Simon and Andrew obeyed at once without demur. If we would always, punctually and with resolute zeal, put in practice what we hear upon the spot, or at the first fit occasion, our attendance at the means of grace, and our reading of good books, could not fail to enrich us spiritually. He will not lose his loaf who has taken care at once to eat it, neither can he be deprived of the benefit of the doctrine who has already acted upon it. Most readers and hearers become moved so far as to purpose to amend; but, alas! the proposal is a blossom which has not been knit, and therefore no fruit comes of it; they wait, they waver, and then they forget, till, like the ponds in nights of frost, when the sun shines by day, they are only thawed in time to be frozen again. That fatal *tomorrow* is blood-red with the murder of fair resolutions; it is the slaughter-house of the innocents. We are very concerned that our little book of "Evening Readings" should not be fruitless, and therefore we pray that readers may not be readers only, but doers, of the word.[1] *The practice of truth is the most profitable reading of it.*

Should the reader be impressed with any duty while perusing these pages, let him hasten to fulfil it before the holy glow has departed from his soul, and let him leave his nets, and all that he has, sooner than be found rebellious to the Master's call. Do not give place to the devil by delay! Haste while opportunity and quickening are in happy conjunction. Do not be caught in your own nets, but break the meshes of worldliness, and away where glory calls you. Happy is the writer who shall meet with readers resolved to carry out his teachings: his harvest shall be a hundredfold, and his Master shall have great honor. Would to God that such might be our reward upon these brief meditations and hurried hints. Grant it, O Lord, unto thy servant! (Spurgeon, pp. Eve, Jun 20)

Footnote:
1. James 1:22.

8

Reading: Luke 3

"The voice of one crying in the wilderness, 'Prepare ye the way of the Lord, make his paths straight.'" Luke 3:4 (AKJV)

The voice crying in the wilderness demanded *a way for the Lord, a way prepared, and a way prepared in the wilderness.* I would be attentive to the Master's proclamation, and give him a road into my heart, cast up by gracious operations, through the desert of my nature. The four directions in the text must have my serious attention.

Every valley must be exalted. Low and groveling thoughts of God must be given up; doubting and despairing must be removed; and self-seeking and carnal delights must be forsaken. Across these deep valleys a glorious causeway of grace must be raised.

Every mountain and hill shall be laid low. Proud creature-sufficiency, and boastful self-righteousness, must be levelled, to make a highway for the King of kings. Divine fellowship is never vouchsafed to haughty, high-minded sinners. The Lord hath respect unto the lowly, and visits the contrite in heart, but the lofty are an abomination unto him. My soul, beseech the Holy Spirit to set thee right in this respect.

The crooked shall be made straight. The wavering heart must have a straight path of decision for God and holiness marked out for it. Double-minded men are strangers to the God of truth. My soul, take heed that thou be in all things honest and true, as in the sight of the heart-searching God.

The rough places shall be made smooth. Stumbling-blocks of sin must be removed, and thorns and briers of rebellion must be uprooted. So great a visitor must not find miry ways and stony places when he comes to honor his favored ones with his company. Oh that this evening the Lord may find in my heart a highway made ready by his grace, that he may make a triumphal progress through the utmost bounds of my soul, from the beginning of this year even to the end of it.[1] (Spurgeon, p. Evening Jan 3)

Footnote:
1. Refer to Isaiah 40:4 for the main points of the devotional.

9

Reading: Matthew 3

"... and he saw the Spirit of God descending like a dove ..." Matthew 3:16

As the Spirit of God descended upon the Lord Jesus, the head, so he also, in measure, descends upon the members of the mystical body. His descent is to us after the same fashion as that in which it fell upon our Lord. There is often a singular rapidity about it; or ever we are aware, we are impelled onward and heavenward beyond all expectation. Yet is there none of the hurry of earthly haste, for the wings of the dove are as soft as they are swift. Quietness seems essential to many spiritual operations; the Lord is in the still small voice,[1] and like the dew, his grace is distilled in silence. The dove has ever been the chosen type of purity, and the Holy Spirit is holiness itself. Where he cometh, everything that is pure and lovely, and of good report, is made to abound, and sin and uncleanness depart. Peace reigns also where the Holy Dove comes with power; he bears the olive branch which shows that the waters of divine wrath are assuaged. Gentleness is a sure result of the Sacred Dove's transforming power: hearts touched by his benign influence are meek and lowly henceforth and forever. Harmlessness follows, as a matter of course; eagles and ravens may hunt their prey – the turtledove can endure wrong, but cannot inflict it. We must be harmless as doves. The dove is an apt picture of love, the voice of the turtle is full of affection; and so, the soul visited by the blessed Spirit, abounds in love to God, in love to the brethren, and in love to sinners; and above all, in love to Jesus. The brooding of the Spirit of God upon the face of the deep, first produced order and life,[2] and in our hearts, he causes and fosters new life and light. Blessed Spirit, as thou didst rest upon our dear Redeemer, even so rest upon us from this time forward and forever. (Spurgeon, p. Evening Mar 3)

Footnotes:
1. 1 Kings 19:11-13.
2. Genesis 1:1-2.

10

Reading: John 1:15-51

"Indeed, we have all received grace upon grace from his fullness." John 1:16

These words tell us that there is a fulness in Christ. There is a fulness of essential Deity, for "in him dwelleth all the fulness of the Godhead."[1] There is a fulness of perfect manhood, for in him, bodily, that Godhead was revealed. There is a fulness of atoning efficacy in his blood, for "the blood of Jesus Christ, his Son, cleanseth us from all sin."[2] There is a fulness of justifying righteousness in his life, for "there is therefore now no condemnation to them that are in Christ Jesus."[3] There is a fulness of divine prevalence in his plea, for "He is able to save to the uttermost them that come unto God by him; seeing he ever liveth to make intercession for them."[4] There is a fulness of victory in his death, for through death he destroyed him that had the power of death, that is the devil. There is a fulness of efficacy in his resurrection from the dead, for by it "we are begotten again unto a lively hope."[5] There is a fulness of triumph in his ascension, for "when he ascended up on high, he led captivity captive, and received gifts for men."[6] There is a fulness of blessings of every sort and shape; a fulness of grace to pardon, of grace to regenerate, of grace to sanctify, of grace to preserve, and of grace to perfect. There is a fulness at all times; a fulness of comfort in affliction; a fulness of guidance in prosperity. A fulness of every divine attribute, of wisdom, of power, of love; a fulness which it were impossible to survey, much less to explore. "It pleased the Father that in him should *all* fulness dwell."[7] Oh, what a fulness must this be of which *all* receive! Fulness, indeed, must there be when the stream is always flowing, and yet the well springs up as free, as rich, as full as ever. Come, believer, and get all thy need supplied; ask largely, and thou shalt receive largely, for this "fulness" is inexhaustible, and is treasured up where all the needy may reach it, even in Jesus, Immanuel – God with us. (Spurgeon, pp. Morning, Jan 27)

Footnotes:
1. Colossians 2:9.
2. 1 John 1:7.
3. Romans 8:1.
4. Hebrews 7:25.
5. 1 Peter 1:3.
6. Ephesians 4:8.
7. Colossians 1:19.

11

Reading: Matthew 4

"Then Jesus was led up by the Spirit into the wilderness to be tempted by the devil." Matthew 4:1

A holy character does not avert temptation – Jesus was tempted. When Satan tempts us, his sparks fall upon tinder; but in Christ's case, it was like striking sparks on water; yet the enemy continued his evil work. Now, if the devil goes on striking when there is no result, how much more will he do it when he knows what inflammable stuff our hearts are made of. Though you become greatly sanctified by the Holy Spirit, expect that the great dog of hell will bark at you still. In the haunts of men, we expect to be tempted, but even seclusion will not guard us from the same trial. Jesus Christ was led away from human society into the wilderness, and was tempted of the devil. Solitude has its charms and its benefits, and may be useful in checking the lust of the eye and the pride of life; but the devil will follow us into the most lovely retreats. Do not suppose that it is only the worldly-minded who have dreadful thoughts and blasphemous temptations, for even spiritual-minded persons endure the same; and in the holiest position we may suffer the darkest temptation. The utmost consecration of spirit will not insure you against Satanic temptation. Christ was consecrated through and through. It was his meat and drink to do the will of him that sent him:[1] and yet he was tempted! Your hearts may glow with a seraphic flame of love to Jesus, and yet the devil will try to bring you down to Laodicean lukewarmness. If you will tell me when God permits a Christian to lay aside his armor,[2] I will tell you when Satan has left off temptation. Like the old knights in war time, we must sleep with helmet and breastplate buckled on, for the arch-deceiver will seize our first unguarded hour to make us his prey. The Lord keep us watchful in all seasons, and give us a final escape from the jaw of the lion and the paw of the bear. (Spurgeon, pp. Eve, Feb 20)

Footnotes:
1. John 4:34.
2. Ephesians 6:10-20.

12

Reading: Luke 4

"*To preach deliverance to the captives.*" Luke 4:18 (AKJV)

None but Jesus can give deliverance to captives. Real liberty cometh from him only. It is a liberty righteously bestowed; for the Son, who is Heir of all things,[1] has a right to make men free. The saints honor the justice of God, which now secures their salvation. It is a liberty which has been dearly purchased. Christ speaks it by his power, but he bought it by his blood. He makes thee free, but it is by his own bonds. Thou goest clear, because he bore thy burden for thee: thou art set at liberty, because he has suffered in thy stead. But, though dearly purchased, he freely gives it. Jesus asks nothing of us as a preparation for this liberty. He finds us sitting in sackcloth and ashes, and bids us put on the beautiful array of freedom; he saves us just as we are, and all without our help or merit. When Jesus sets free, the liberty is perpetually entailed; no chains can bind again. Let the Master say to me, "Captive, I have delivered thee," and it is done for ever. Satan may plot to enslave us, but if the Lord be on our side, whom shall we fear?[2] The world, with its temptations, may seek to ensnare us, but mightier is he who is for us than all they who be against us. The machinations of our own deceitful hearts may harass and annoy us, but he who hath begun the good work in us will carry it on and perfect it to the end.[3] The foes of God and the enemies of man may gather their hosts together, and come with concentrated fury against us, but if God acquitteth, who is he that condemneth?[4] Not more free is the eagle which mounts to his rocky eyrie, and afterwards outsoars the clouds, than the soul which Christ hath delivered. If we are no more under the law, but free from its curse, let our liberty be practically exhibited in our serving God with gratitude and delight. "I am thy servant, and the son of thine handmaid: thou hast loosed my bonds."[5] "Lord, what wilt thou have me to do?"[6] (Spurgeon, p. Morning Nov 25)

Footnotes:
1. Romans 8:17.
2. Psalm 27:1.
3. Philippians 1:6.
4. Romans 8:34.
5. Psalm 116:16.
6. Acts 9:6.

13

Reading: Luke 5

"*Launch out into the deep, and let down your nets for a draught.*" Luke 5:4 (AKJV)

We learn from this narrative, *the necessity of human agency.* The draught of fishes was miraculous, yet neither the fisherman nor his boat, nor his fishing tackle were ignored; but all were used to take the fishes. So in the saving of souls, God worketh by means; and while the present economy of grace shall stand, God will be pleased by the foolishness of preaching to save them that believe. When God worketh without instruments, doubtless he is glorified; but he hath himself selected the plan of instrumentality as being that by which he is most magnified in the earth. *Means of themselves are utterly unavailing.* "Master, we have toiled all the night and have taken nothing." What was the reason of this? Were they not fishermen plying their special calling? Verily, they were no raw hands; they understood the work. Had they gone about the toil unskillfully? No. Had they lacked industry? No, they had toiled. Had they lacked perseverance? No, they had *toiled all the night.* Was there a deficiency of fish in the sea? Certainly not, for as soon as the Master came, they swam to the net in shoals. What, then, is the reason? Is it because there is no power in the means of themselves apart from the presence of Jesus? "Without him we can do nothing."[1] But with Christ we can do all things. *Christ's presence confers success.* Jesus sat in Peter's boat, and his will, by a mysterious influence, drew the fish to the net. When Jesus is lifted up in his Church, his presence is the Church's power – the shout of a king is in the midst of her. "I, if I be lifted up, will draw all men unto me."[2] Let us go out this morning on our work of soul fishing, looking up in faith, and around us in solemn anxiety. Let us toil till night comes, and we shall not labor in vain, for he who bids us let down the net, will fill it with fishes. (Spurgeon, p. Morning Oct 8)

Footnotes:
1. John 15:5.
2. John 12:32.

14

Reading: John 2

"Jesus answered, "Destroy this temple, and I will raise it up in three days." ... But he was speaking about the temple of his body." John 2:19, 21

This temple was to be destroyed. Jesus must die! This was the second step in the accomplishment of the great work. Thus did He announce the fact to the obtuse and incredulous Jews "Destroy this temple, and in three days I will raise it up." His death was as necessary to the satisfaction of justice, as His life of obedience had been to the fulfilling of the law. As the substitute of His people, He must yield up His life; as the Surety of the covenant, He must completely surrender Himself into the hands of Divine justice; as the Testator of His own will, there must of necessity be His death, Otherwise the testament would have been of no force at all while He lived. There was no possible avenue for His escape, even had He sought it. He, or His people, must die. He must taste the bitterness of the death that was temporal, or His elect must have tasted of the bitterness of the death that was eternal. Oh yes, Jesus wished to die. Never for one moment did He really shrink from the combat. He well knew the conditions upon which He had entered into a covenant engagement in behalf of His people. He knew that the price of their pardon was His own blood,[1] that His death was their life, and that His gloomy path through the grave was their bright passage to eternal glory. Knowing all this, and with the awful scene of Calvary full in view – the cross, the sufferings of the body, the deathly sorrow of the soul – He yet panted for the arrival of the moment that was to finish the work His Father had given Him to do.

Dear reader, how ready was Jesus thus to die! Where this eagerness? It sprang from His great love to sinners. Oh, this was it! We must go down to the secret depth of His love, if we would solve the mystery of His willingness to die. "God commends His love toward us, in that while we were yet sinners, Christ died for us."[2] Thus was the "temple of His body" destroyed, that "through death He might destroy him that had the power of death, that is, the devil, and deliver them who through fear of death were all their lifetime subject to bondage."[3] See, dear reader, the source of your free pardon, the ground of your humble trust, the secret of your "strong consolation." It is all involved in the death of Jesus. You cannot ask too much, you cannot expect too much, you cannot repose too much at the foot of the cross. All is mercy here – all is love – all is peace. Sin cannot condemn, Satan cannot tempt, the world cannot allure, conscience cannot accuse; "there is no condemnation"[4] to a poor soul that shelters itself beneath the cross of Jesus. Here every dark cloud withdraws, and all is sunny – here every tear is dried, but that of joy, and every voice is hushed, but that of praise. (Winslow, Evening Thoughts, p. May 5)

Footnotes:
1. Hebrews 10:12.
2. Romans 5:8.
3. Hebrews 2:14-15.
4. Romans 8:1.

15

Reading: John 3

"The Son of man." John 3:13

How constantly our Master used the title, the "Son of man!" If he had chosen, he might always have spoken of himself as the Son of God, the Everlasting Father, the Wonderful, the Counsellor, the Prince of Peace;[1] but behold the lowliness of Jesus! He prefers to call himself the Son of man. Let us learn a lesson of humility from our Savior; let us never court great titles nor proud degrees. There is here, however, a far sweeter thought. Jesus loved manhood so much, that he delighted to honor it; and since it is a high honor, and indeed, the greatest dignity of manhood, that Jesus is the Son of man, he is wont to display this name, that he may as it were hang royal stars upon the breast of manhood, and show forth the love of God to Abraham's seed. *Son of man* – whenever he said that word, he shed a halo round the head of Adam's children. Yet there is perhaps a more precious thought still. Jesus Christ called himself the Son of man to express his oneness and sympathy with his people. He thus reminds us that he is the one whom we may approach without fear. As a man, we may take to him all our griefs and troubles, for he knows them by experience; in that he himself hath suffered as the "Son of man," he is able to succor and comfort us. All hail, thou blessed Jesus! inasmuch as thou art evermore using the sweet name which acknowledges that thou art a brother and a near kinsman, it is to us a dear token of thy grace, thy humility, thy love.

> *"Oh see how Jesus trusts himself*
> *Unto our childish love,*
> *As though by his free ways with us*
> *Our earnestness to prove!*
> *His sacred name a common word*
> *On earth he loves to hear;*
> *There is no majesty in him*
> *Which love may not come near."*
> (Spurgeon, pp. Eve, Mar 25)

Footnote:
1. Isaiah 9:6.

16

Reading: John 4

"But whoever drinks from the water that I will give him will never get thirsty again..." John 4:14

He who is a believer in Jesus finds enough in his Lord to satisfy him now, and to content him for evermore. The believer is not the man whose days are weary for want of comfort, and whose nights are long from absence of heart-cheering thought, for he finds in religion such a spring of joy, such a fountain of consolation, that he is content and happy. Put him in a dungeon and he will find good company; place him in a barren wilderness, he will eat the bread of heaven; drive him away from friendship, he will meet the "friend that sticketh closer than a brother."[1] Blast all his gourds, and he will find shadow beneath the Rock of Ages; sap the foundation of his earthly hopes, but his heart will still be fixed, trusting in the Lord. The heart is as insatiable as the grave till Jesus enters it, and then it is a cup full to overflowing. There is such a fulness in Christ that he alone is the believer's all. The true saint is so completely satisfied with the all-sufficiency of Jesus that he thirsts no more – except it be for deeper draughts of the living fountain. In that sweet manner, believer, shalt thou thirst; it shall not be a thirst of pain, but of loving desire; thou wilt find it a sweet thing to be panting after a fuller enjoyment of Jesus' love. One in days of yore said, "I have been sinking my bucket down into the well full often, but now my thirst after Jesus has become so insatiable, that I long to put the well itself to my lips, and drink right on." Is this the feeling of thine heart now, believer? Dost thou feel that all thy desires are satisfied in Jesus, and that thou hast no want now, but to know more of him, and to have closer fellowship with him? Then come continually to the fountain, and take of the water of life freely. Jesus will never think you take too much, but will ever welcome you, saying, "Drink, yea, drink abundantly, O beloved."[2] (Spurgeon, pp. Morning, Oct 6)

Footnotes:
1. Proverbs 18:24.
2. Song of Songs / Solomon 5:1.

17

Reading: Mark 2

"Since they were not able to bring him to Jesus because of the crowd, they removed the roof above him, and after digging through it, they lowered the mat on which the paralytic was lying." Mark 2:4

Faith is full of inventions. The house was full, a crowd blocked up the door, but faith found a way of getting at the Lord and placing the palsied man before him. If we cannot get sinners where Jesus is by ordinary methods, we must use extraordinary ones. It seems, according to Luke 5:19, that a tiling had to be removed, which would make dust and cause a measure of danger to those below, but where the case is very urgent, we must not mind running some risks and shocking some proprieties. Jesus was there to heal, and therefore fall what might, faith ventured all so that her poor paralyzed charge might have his sins forgiven. O that we had more daring faith among us! Cannot we, dear reader, seek it this morning for ourselves and for our fellow-workers, and will we not try today to perform some gallant act for the love of souls and the glory of the Lord.

The world is constantly inventing; genius serves all the purposes of human desire: cannot faith invent too, and reach by some new means the outcasts who lie perishing around us? It was the presence of Jesus which excited victorious courage in the four bearers of the palsied man: is not the Lord among us now? Have we seen his face for ourselves this morning? Have we felt his healing power in our own souls? If so, then through door, through window, or through roof, let us, breaking through all impediments, labor to bring poor souls to Jesus. All means are good and decorous when faith and love are truly set on winning souls. If hunger for bread can break through stone walls, surely hunger for souls is not to be hindered in its efforts. O Lord, make us quick to suggest methods of reaching thy poor sin-sick ones, and bold to carry them out at all hazards. (Spurgeon, p. Morning Sep 7)

18

Reading: John 5

"Search the Scriptures." John 5:39 (AKJV)

The Greek word here rendered search signifies a strict, close, diligent, curious search, such as men make when they are seeking gold, or hunters when they are in earnest after game. We must not rest content with having given a superficial reading to a chapter or two, but with the candle of the Spirit we must deliberately seek out the hidden meaning of the word. Holy Scripture *requires searching* – much of it can only be learned by careful study. There is milk for babes, but also meat for strong men.[1] The rabbis wisely say that a mountain of matter hangs upon every word, yea, upon every title of Scripture. Tertullian exclaims, "I adore the fulness of the Scriptures." No man who merely skims the book of God can profit thereby; we must dig and mine until we obtain the hid treasure. The door of the word only opens to the key of diligence. The Scriptures *claim searching*. They are the writings of God, bearing the divine stamp and imprimatur[2] – who shall dare to treat them with levity? He who despises them despises the God who wrote them. God forbid that any of us should leave our Bibles to become swift witnesses against us in the great day of account. The word of God will *repay searching*. God does not bid us sift a mountain of chaff with here and there a grain of wheat in it, but the Bible is winnowed corn – we have but to open the granary door and find it. Scripture grows upon the student. It is full of surprises. Under the teaching of the Holy Spirit, to the searching eye it glows with splendor of revelation, like a vast temple paved with wrought gold, and roofed with rubies, emeralds, and all manner of gems. No merchandise like the merchandise of Scripture truth. Lastly, *the Scriptures reveal Jesus*: "They are they which testify of me."[3] No more powerful motive can be urged upon Bible readers than this: he who finds Jesus finds life, heaven, all things. Happy he who, searching his Bible, discovers his Savior. (Spurgeon, p. Evening Jun 9)

Footnotes:
1. 1 Peter 2:2; 1 Corinthians 3:2.
2. Timothy 3:16.
3. John 5:39; John 5:46.

19

Reading: Mark 3

"Jesus went up the mountain and summoned those he wanted, and they came to him." Mark 3:13

Here was sovereignty. Impatient spirits may fret and fume, because they are not called to the highest places in the ministry; but reader be it thine to rejoice that Jesus calleth whom he wills. If he shall leave me to be a doorkeeper in his house,[1] I will cheerfully bless him for his grace in permitting me to do anything in his service. The call of Christ's servants comes from above. Jesus stands on the mountain, evermore above the world in holiness, earnestness, love and power. Those whom he calls must go up the mountain to him, they must seek to rise to his level by living in constant communion with him. They may not be able to mount to classic honors, or attain scholastic eminence, but they must like Moses go up into the mount of God and have familiar intercourse with the unseen God, or they will never be fitted to proclaim the gospel of peace. Jesus went apart to hold high fellowship with the Father, and we must enter into the same divine companionship if we would bless our fellowmen. No wonder that the apostles were clothed with power when they came down fresh from the mountain where Jesus was. This morning we must endeavor to ascend the mount of communion, that there we may be ordained to the lifework for which we are set apart. Let us not see the face of man today till we have seen Jesus. Time spent with him is laid out at blessed interest. We too shall cast out devils and work wonders if we go down into the world girded with that divine energy which Christ alone can give. It is of no use going to the Lord's battle till we are armed with heavenly weapons. We must see Jesus, this is essential. At the mercy-seat we will linger till he shall manifest himself unto us as he doth not unto the world, and until we can truthfully say, "We were with him in the Holy Mount."[2] (Spurgeon, p. Morning Sep 10)

Footnotes:
1. Psalm 84:10.
2. 2 Peter 1:18.

20

Reading: Luke 6

"During those days he went out to the mountain to pray and spent all night in prayer to God." Luke 6:12

If ever one of woman born might have lived without prayer, it was our spotless, perfect Lord, and yet none was ever so much in supplication as he! Such was his love to his Father, that he loved much to be in communion with him: such his love for his people, that he desired to be much in intercession for them. *The fact* of this eminent prayerfulness of Jesus is a lesson for us – he hath given us an example that we may follow in his steps. *The time* he chose was admirable, it was the hour of silence, when the crowd would not disturb him; the time of inaction, when all but himself had ceased to labor; and the season when slumber made men forget their woes, and cease their applications to him for relief. While others found rest in sleep, he refreshed himself with prayer. *The place* was also well selected. He was alone where none would intrude, where none could observe: thus was he free from Pharisaic ostentation and vulgar interruption. Those dark and silent hills were a fit oratory for the Son of God. Heaven and earth in midnight stillness heard the groans and sighs of the mysterious Being in whom both worlds were blended. *The continuance* of his pleadings is remarkable; the long watches were not too long; the cold wind did not chill his devotions; the grim darkness did not darken his faith, or loneliness check his importunity. We cannot watch with him one hour, but he watched for us whole nights. *The occasion* for this prayer is notable; it was after his enemies had been enraged – prayer was his refuge and solace; it was before he sent forth the twelve apostles – prayer was the gate of his enterprise, the herald of his new work. Should we not learn from Jesus to resort to special prayer when we are under peculiar trial, or contemplate fresh endeavors for the Master's glory? Lord Jesus, teach us to pray.[1] (Spurgeon, p. Evening Nov 12)

Footnote:
1. Luke 11:1.

21

Reading: Matthew 12:1-21

"*A bruised reed shall he not break, and smoking flax shall he not quench.*" Matthew 12:20

What is weaker than the bruised reed or the smoking flax? A *reed* that groweth in the fen or marsh, let but the wild duck light upon it, and it snaps; let but the foot of man brush against it, and it is bruised and broken; every wind that flits across the river moves it to and fro. You can conceive of nothing more frail or brittle, or whose existence is more in jeopardy, than a bruised reed. Then look at the smoking flax – what is it? It has a spark within it, it is true, but it is almost smothered; an infant's breath might blow it out; nothing has a more precarious existence than its flame. *Weak things* are here described, yet Jesus says of them, "The smoking flax I will not quench; the bruised reed I will not break." Some of God's children are made strong to do mighty works for him; God has his Samsons here and there who can pull up Gaza's gates, and carry them to the top of the hill;[1] he has a few mighties who are lion-like men, but the majority of his people are a timid, trembling race. They are like starlings, frightened at every passerby; a little fearful flock. If temptation comes, they are taken like birds in a snare; if trial threatens, they are ready to faint; their frail skiff is tossed up and down by every wave, they are drifted along like a sea bird on the crest of the billows – weak things, without strength, without wisdom, without foresight. Yet, weak as they are, and *because* they are so weak, they have this promise made specially to them. Herein is grace and graciousness! Herein is love and lovingkindness! How it opens to us the compassion of Jesus – so gentle, tender, considerate! We need never shrink back from *his* touch. We need never fear a harsh word from *him*; though he might well chide us for our weakness, he rebuketh not. Bruised reeds shall have no blows from him, and the smoking flax no damping frowns. (Spurgeon, p. Evening Jul 19)

Footnote:
1. Judges, chapter 16.

22

Reading: Matthew 5

"... Love your neighbor ..." Matthew 5:43

"Love thy neighbor." Perhaps he rolls in riches, and thou art poor, and living in thy little cot side-by-side with his lordly mansion; thou seest every day his estates, his fine linen, and his sumptuous banquets; God has given him these gifts, covet not his wealth, and think no hard thoughts concerning him. Be content with thine own lot, if thou canst not better it, but do not look upon thy neighbor, and wish that he were as thyself. Love him, and then thou wilt not envy him.

Perhaps, on the other hand, thou art rich, and near thee reside the poor. Do not scorn to call them neighbor. Own that thou art bound to love them. The world calls them thy inferiors. In what are they inferior? They are far more thine equals than thine inferiors, for "God hath made of one blood all people that dwell upon the face of the earth."[1] It is thy coat which is better than theirs, but thou art by no means better than they. They are men, and what art thou more than that? Take heed that thou love thy neighbor even though he be in rags, or sunken in the depths of poverty.

But, perhaps, you say, "I cannot love my neighbors, because for all I do they return ingratitude and contempt." So much the more room for the heroism of love. Wouldst thou be a feather-bed warrior, instead of bearing the rough fight of love? He who dares the most, shall win the most; and if rough be thy path of love, tread it boldly, still loving thy neighbors through thick and thin. Heap coals of fire on their heads, and if they be hard to please, seek not to please *them*, but to please *thy Master*; and remember if *they* spurn thy love, thy Master hath not spurned it, and thy deed is as acceptable to him as if it had been acceptable to them. Love thy neighbor, for in so doing thou art following the footsteps of Christ. (Spurgeon, pp. Morning, Mar 12)

Footnote:
1. Acts 17:26.

23

Reading: Matthew 6

"Your heavenly Father." Matthew 6:26

God's people are doubly his children, they are his offspring by creation, and they are his sons by adoption in Christ. Hence, they are privileged to call him, "Our Father which art in heaven." Father! Oh, what precious word is that. Here is *authority*: "If I be a Father, where is mine honor?"[1] If ye be sons, where is your obedience? Here is *affection* mingled with authority; an authority which does not provoke rebellion; an obedience demanded which is most cheerfully rendered – which would not be withheld even if it might. The obedience which God's children yield to him must be *loving* obedience. Do not go about the service of God as slaves to their taskmaster's toil, but run in the way of his commands because it is your *Father's* way. Yield your bodies as instruments of righteousness, because righteousness is your Father's will, and his will should be the will of his child. *Father!* – Here is a kingly attribute so sweetly veiled in love, that the King's crown is forgotten in the King's face, and his scepter becomes, not a rod of iron, but a silver scepter of mercy – the scepter indeed seems to be forgotten in the tender hand of him who wields it. Father! – Here is honor and love. How great is a Father's love to his children![2] That which friendship cannot do, and mere benevolence will not attempt, a father's heart and hand must do for his sons. They are his offspring, he must bless them; they are his children, he must show himself strong in their defense. If an earthly father watches over his children with unceasing love and care, how much more does our heavenly Father? Abba, Father! He who can say this, hath uttered better music than cherubim or seraphim can reach. There is heaven in the depth of that word – Father! There is all I can ask; all my necessities can demand; all my wishes can desire. I have all in all to all eternity when I can say, "Father." (Spurgeon, p. Morning Jan 26)

Footnotes:
1. Malachi 1:6.
2. 1 John 3:1.

24

Reading: Matthew 7

Reader! having gone over the whole of this blessed Sermon of Christ, let us sum up the contents, and beg of God the Holy Spirit to write all the gracious truths contained in it in our hearts. And while we hear the Lord giving to his Church the whole Gospel of Salvation, oh! what a blessed consideration is it, that Jesus himself hath fulfilled all,[1] and is all to his redeemed. Never may the Church of Jesus forget this, but receive Christ as the Father's gift, and the complete salvation of Jehovah to the end of the earth!

Precious, blessed Lord Jesus! so may my soul hear these sayings of thine, and embrace them, that building upon thee as the foundation, the superstructure, and the whole, both of Law and the Prophets, when, the Lord shall arise to shake terribly the earth, I may be found firm on the rock, *against which the gates of hell shall never prevail.*[2] Despised as thou hast been, and still art, by Jews and false Christians, and a stone of stumbling and rock of offence;[3] yet to me be thou more precious than the mountains of spices. In thy person, work and offices; in thy character and relations; in thy complete righteousness and salvation; be thou my Lord, my hope, and everlasting portion. Lord grant that I may never build on the sandy performance of anything of my own, or mix up with thy complete work the hay and the stubble of any legal righteousness, which can stand no wind of the day of God's wrath; but be thou the all in all, of all grace here, and of glory forever. Amen. (Hawker, Poor Man's New Testament Commentary: Matthew-John, pp. 53–54)

Footnotes:
1. Matthew 5:17-19; Galatians 5:14.
2. Matthew 16:18.
3. 1 Corinthians 1:23.

25

Reading: Luke 7

"Do you see this woman?" Luke 7:44

My soul! look at this woman at the feet of Jesus; for thy Jesus bids thee look, and gather instruction from the view as well as the Pharisee. Behold how she wept, how she washed the feet of Jesus, and anointed them with ointment. These were sweet tokens of her love and adoration. But were these the causes for which she obtained forgiveness? Oh! no. Read what the Lord said to her: — "Thy faith hath saved thee."[1] Learn then, my soul, in what salvation lies. Love may bring ointment to Jesus. Sorrow for sin, when grace is in the heart, will cause tears to fall. But faith brings nothing; for it hath nothing. It casts itself wholly upon Jesus. Amidst all its guilt, and fears, and tears, it is Jesus only to whom faith looks. It is Jesus upon whom alone it depends. It hath nothing to do with self; neither our own feelings, nor the exercise of our graces. These are blessed evidences of the work of the Lord upon the heart: but they are not salvation. It is Jesus, all precious, all glorious, all suitable Jesus! He is the one blessed object of faith's joy, and hope, and pursuit, and desire. And depend upon it, thy God and Father in Christ

Jesus is more pleased, more honored by this simple act of faith upon Jesus' glorious person and righteousness, than by all the tears in the world; when those tears lead us to place a stress upon the *effects* of faith, instead of hanging wholly upon the *cause*, in the glorious object, Jesus. Pause, my soul, over this nice but proper distinction; and this will be to find comfort always in Jesus. "Seest thou this woman?" (Hawker, The Poor Man's Morning Portion, p. Feb 2)

Footnote:
1. Matthew 7:50.

26

Reading: Matthew 8:1-13

"Right away a man with leprosy came up and knelt before him, saying, "Lord, if you are willing, you can make me clean." Reaching out his hand, Jesus touched him, saying, "I am willing; be made clean." Immediately his leprosy was cleansed." Matthew 8:2-3

Behold, my soul, in the instance of this leper, thine own circumstances. What he was in body, such wert thou in soul. As his leprosy made him loathsome and offensive before men, so thy polluted soul made thee odious in the sight of God. He would not have sought a cure, had he not been conscious of his need of it. Neither wouldest thou have ever looked to Jesus, had he not convinced thee of thy helplessness and misery without him. Moreover, he would not, though convinced how much he needed healing, have sought that mercy from Jesus, had he not been made sensible of Jesus' ability to the cure. Neither wouldest thou ever have come to Jesus, hadst thou not been taught who Jesus is, and how fully competent to deliver thee. The poor leper did not doubt whether Jesus was able; though he rather feared that ability might not be exercised towards him. His prayer was, not if thou art *able*; but, "Lord, if thou *wilt*, thou canst make me clean." Now here, my soul, I hope thy faith, through grace, exceeds the Jewish leper. Surely, thou both knowest Jesus' power and Jesus' disposition to save thee. Unworthy and undeserving as thou art, yet his grace is not restrained by thy undeservings, no more than it was first constrained by thy merit. His love, his own love, his free love, is the sole rule of his mercy towards his children, and not their claims; for they have none, but in his free grace and the Father's everlasting mercy.[1] Cherish these thoughts, my soul, at all times, for they are most sweet and precious. But are these all the blessed things which arise out of the view of the poor leper's case? Oh! no; the most delightful part still remains in the contemplation of Jesus' mercy to the poor petitioner, and the very gracious manner the Son of God manifested in the bestowing of it. He not only healed him, and did it immediately, but with that tenderness which distinguished his character and his love to poor sinners, Jesus put forth his hand and touched him: touched a leper. Even so, precious Lord! deal by me. Though polluted and unclean, yet condescend to put forth thine hand and touch me also. Put forth thy blessed Spirit. Come, Lord, and dwell in me, abide in me, and rule and reign over me. Be thou my God, my Jesus, my Holy One, and make me thine forever? (Hawker, The Poor Man's Morning Portion, p. Mar 11)

Footnote:
1. 1 John 4:19; Romans 5:8.

27

Reading: Matthew 11

"Come to me." Matthew 11:28

The cry of the Christian religion is the gentle word, "Come." The Jewish law harshly said, "Go, take heed unto thy steps as to the path in which thou shalt walk. Break the commandments, and thou shalt perish; keep them, and thou shalt live." The law was a dispensation of terror, which drove men before it as with a scourge; the gospel draws with bands of love. Jesus is the good Shepherd[1] going before his sheep, bidding them follow him, and ever leading them onwards with the sweet word, "Come." The law repels, the gospel attracts. The law shows the distance which there is between God and man; the gospel bridges that awful chasm, and brings the sinner across it.

From the first moment of your spiritual life until you are ushered into glory, the language of Christ to you will be, *"Come, come unto me."* As a mother puts out her finger to her little child and woos it to walk by saying, *"Come,"* even so does Jesus. He will always be ahead of you, bidding you follow him as the soldier follows his captain. He will always go before you to pave your way, and clear your path, and you shall hear his animating voice calling you after him all through life; while in the solemn hour of death, his sweet words with which he shall usher you into the heavenly world shall be – "Come, ye blessed of my Father."[2]

Nay, further, this is not only Christ's cry to you, but, if you be a believer, this is your cry to Christ – "Come! come!" You will be longing for his second advent; you will be saying, "Come quickly, even so come Lord Jesus."[3] You will be panting for nearer and closer communion with him. As his voice to you is "Come," your response to him will be, "Come, Lord, and abide with me. Come, and occupy alone the throne of my heart; reign there without a rival, and consecrate me entirely to thy service." (Spurgeon, p. Morning Dec 16)

Footnotes:
1. John 10:11-18.
2. Matthew 25:34.
3. Revelation 22:20.

28

Reading: Matthew 12:22-50

"... Stretching out his hand toward his disciples, he said, 'Here are my mother and my brothers!" Matthew 12:49

It is a matter of no small importance in the faith of every child of God, to have right apprehensions of our Lord's relations after the flesh. As *Joseph* was only the reputed father of Christ (and not in reality), very plain it is, that on this side Jesus had none. And whether the Virgin *Mary* had, or had not children after the birth of Christ, it is of no moment to enquire, for it forms no article of faith: neither is it in the least connected with the present question. That *Mary* was a pure Virgin, at the time of her conception; that she continued so, to the birth of Christ; and that her conception, was altogether miraculous, by the Holy Spirit, and without the intervention of an human father: these are the grand and the only points essential to be proved; and these are all most fully proved and ascertained in the scriptures. And hence it will follow, that any further relationship after the flesh, Christ had none. But his brethren are the members of this *mystical* body, and not his *personal* body. Christ and his seed, are spoken of as one. He the head, and they the members; and concerning whom Jehovah saith, *I will pour my spirit upon thy seed, and my blessing upon thine offspring.*[1] In that holy portion of human nature which constituted Christ's body, underived from man, and given of God, from all the persons of the Godhead:[2] was formed the holy seed, of all his members. And as it is said of *Levi*, that he was in the loins of his father, when *Melchisedek* met him;[3] so must it be said of the seed of Christ: they were in Christ; chosen in Christ; blessed in Christ; yea, beheld in Christ, *before the world began.*[4] So that when the Lord Jesus, in answer to the person, speaking to him of his relations, as stated in this Chapter, stretched forth his hand towards his disciples, and pointing to certain among the throng, and said, *behold my Mother and my Brethren!* these were, Christ's relations both in nature and grace. And if the Reader will turn to the following scriptures in proof, they will serve to throw great light upon the subject. As the everlasting *Father, Brother, Husband, Friend.*[5] See the Poor Man's Commentary also on [Matthew] Chapter 1 verse 22–25. (Hawker, Poor Man's New Testament Commentary: Matthew-John, pp. 90–91)

Footnotes:
1. Isaiah 44:3; Isaiah 59:21.
2. See in proof, Psalms 40:6. Hebrews 10:5. Psalms 139:13–16. Hebrews 2:14–16; Luke 1:35 and Poor Man's Commentary on Matthew 1:18.
3. Hebrews 7:10.
4. Ephesians 1:3-5; Isaiah 8:18; Hebrews 2:11.
5. Isaiah 9:6; John 20:17; Isaiah 54:5; John 15:15.

29

Reading: Luke 8

"But as he went." Luke 8:42

Jesus is passing through the throng to the house of Jairus, to raise the ruler's dead daughter; but he is so profuse in goodness that he works another miracle while upon the road. While yet this rod of Aaron bears the blossom of an unaccomplished wonder, it yields the ripe almonds of a perfect work of mercy.[1] It is enough for us, if we have some one purpose, straightway to go and accomplish it; it were imprudent to expend our energies by the way. Hastening to the rescue of a drowning friend, we cannot afford to exhaust our strength upon another in like danger. It is enough for a tree to yield one sort of fruit, and for a man to fulfil his own peculiar calling. But our Master knows no limit of power or boundary of mission. He is so prolific of grace, that like the sun which shines as it rolls onward in its orbit, his path is radiant with lovingkindness. He is a swift arrow of love, which not only reaches its ordained target, but perfumes the air through which it flies. Virtue is evermore going out of Jesus, as sweet odors exhale from flowers; and it always will be emanating from him, as water from a sparkling fountain. What delightful encouragement this truth affords us! If our Lord is so ready to heal the sick and bless the needy, then, my soul, be not thou slow to put thyself in his way, that he may smile on thee. Be not slack in asking, if he be so abundant in bestowing. Give earnest heed to his word now, and at all times, that Jesus may speak through it to thy heart. Where he is to be found there make thy resort, that thou mayst obtain his blessing. When he is present to heal, may he not heal thee? But surely he is present even now, for he always comes to hearts which need him. And dost not thou need him? Ah, he knows how much! Thou Son of David, turn thine eye and look upon the distress which is now before thee, and make thy suppliant whole. (Spurgeon, p. Evening Aug 3)

Footnote:
1. Numbers 17:8.

30

Reading: Matthew 13

"And the one sown on rocky ground – this is one who hears the word and immediately receives it with joy. But he has no root and is short-lived. When distress or persecution comes because of the word, immediately he falls away. Now the one sown among the thorns – this is one who hears the word, but the worries of this age and the deceitfulness of wealth choke the word, and it becomes unfruitful." Matthew 13:20-22

    A season of prosperity often proves fatal to a profession of godliness. Divine providence smiles, riches increase, and with them the temptations and the snares, the luxury, indulgence, and worldly show which are inseparable from the accumulation of unsanctified and unconsecrated wealth. And what are the results? In most cases, the entire relinquishment of the outward garb of a religious costume. Found to be in the way of the full indulgence of the carnal mind, it is laid aside altogether; and thus freed from all the restraints which consistency imposed, the heart at once plunges deep into the world it all the while secretly loved, sighed for, and worshiped. Oh, what a severe but true test of religious principle is this! How soon it detects the spurious and the false! How soon does the verdure wither away! "The prosperity of fools shall destroy them."¹

But if a professing man passes through this trial, and still retains his integrity; still walks closely and humbly with God; still adheres to the lowly cross bearing path of Jesus; is still found as diligent in waiting upon God in public and private means of grace; is still as meek, condescending, and kind, increasing in devotedness, liberality, and love, with the increase of God's providential goodness around him, such a man has the "root of the matter in him;" and "he shall be like a tree planted by the rivers of water, that brings forth his fruit in his season; his leaf also shall not wither; and whatever he does shall prosper."² His prosperity has not destroyed him.

A time of adversity is often equally as fatal to a profession of religion, founded upon no true Christian principle. If in the smooth path we are apt to slide, in the rough path we may stumble. Periods of great revolution in the history of the Christian Church, when God tries the principles, the conscience, the love, and the faith of His people, are test-periods. What numbers make shipwreck then of their high profession! And when God enters the pleasant garden of a man's domestic blessings, and blows upon the lovely blossom, or blights the fair flower, or severs the pleasant bough, or scatters the hard-earned wealth of years, or wastes the body's vigor, or frustrates the fond scheme; how does an unrenewed man behave himself?

Is his carriage humble, submissive, child-like? Does stern Christian principle now exhibit itself, in beautiful contrast with the trial that has called it forth? Does divine grace, like the aromatic flower, now appear the sweeter and more precious for its being crushed? Does not every feeling of the heart rise in maddened rebellion against God and against His government? Ah, yes! How accurately does Christ describe his case: "he has not root in himself, but endures for a while; for when tribulation or persecution arises because of the word, by and by he is offended."[3] (Winslow, Morning Thoughts, p. Aug 29)

Footnotes:
1. Proverbs 1:32.
2. Psalm 1:3.
3. Matthew 13:21.

31

Reading: Mark 4

"Why are you afraid? Do you still have no faith?" Mark 4:40

The habitual, or even the occasional, doubtful apprehension indulged in of his interest in Christ will tend materially to the enfeebling and decay of a believer's faith; no cause can be more certain in its effects than this. If it be true that the exercise of faith develops its strength, it is equally true that the perpetual indulgence of doubtful apprehensions of pardon and acceptance must necessarily eat as a canker-worm at the root of faith. Every misgiving felt, every doubt cherished, every fear yielded to, every dark providence brooded over, tends to unhinge the soul from God, and dims its near and loving view of Jesus. To doubt the love, the wisdom, and the faithfulness of God, to doubt the perfection of the work of Christ, to doubt the operation of the Spirit on the heart, what can tend more to the weakening and decay of this precious and costly grace? Every time the soul sinks under the pressure of a doubt of its interest in Christ, the effect must be a weakening of the soul's view of the glory, perfection, and all-sufficiency of Christ's work. But imperfectly may the doubting Christian be aware what dishonor is done to Jesus, what reflection is cast upon His great work, by every unbelieving fear he cherishes. It is a secret wounding of Jesus, however the soul might shrink from such an inference; it is a lowering, an undervaluing of Christ's obedience and death[1] – that glorious work of salvation with which the Father has declared Himself well pleased – that work with which divine justice has confessed itself satisfied – that work, on the basis of which every poor, convinced sinner is saved, and on the ground of which millions of redeemed and glorified spirits are now basking around the throne – that work, we say, is dishonored, undervalued, and slighted by every doubt and fear secretly harbored or openly expressed by a child of God. The moment a believer looks at his unworthiness more than at the righteousness of Christ – supposes that there is not a sufficiency of merit in Jesus to supply the absence of all merit in himself before God – what is it but a setting up his sinfulness and unworthiness above the infinite worth, fulness, and sufficiency of Christ's atonement and righteousness? There is much spurious humility among many of the dear saints of God. It is thought by some, that to be always doubting one's pardon and acceptance is the evidence of a humble spirit. It is, allow us to say, the mark of the very opposite of a lowly and humble mind. That is true humility that credits the testimony of God – that believes because He has spoken it – that rests in the blood and righteousness and all-sufficiency of Jesus, because He has declared that "whoever believes in Him shall be saved."[2] This is genuine lowliness – the blessed product of the Eternal Spirit. To go to Jesus just as I am, a poor, lost, helpless sinner – to go without previous preparation – to go glorying in my weakness, infirmity, and poverty, that the free grace, and sovereign pleasure, and infinite merit of Christ might be seen in my full pardon, justification, and eternal glory. There is more of unmortified pride, of self-righteousness, of that principle that would make God a debtor to the creature, in the refusal of a soul fully to accept of Jesus, than is suspected. There is more real, profound humility in a simple, believing venture upon Christ, as a ruined sinner, taking Him as all its righteousness, all its pardon, all its glory, than it is possible for any mortal mind to fathom. Doubt is ever the offspring of pride; humility is ever the handmaid of faith. (Winslow, Morning Thoughts, p. May 4)

Footnotes:
1. Philippians 2:8; 1 John 4:9-11.
2. John 3:16-17.

32

Reading: Mark 5

"Only believe." Mark 5:36

Precious and significant are the words of Jesus, the very same words that He spoke when on earth. Did those lips, glowing with more than a seraph's hallowed touch – lips into which grace without measure was poured – ever breathe a sentence more touching, more simple, or more significant than this, "Only believe"? Originally addressed to an afflicted parent, who sought His compassion and His help in behalf of a little daughter lying at the point of death, they seem to be especially appropriate to every case of anxiety, of trial, and of need. Alas! how many such will scan this page – how many a sigh will breathe over it, how many a tear will moisten it, how many a mournful glance will light upon it! Be it so; there comes back a voice of sympathy responsive to each sad heart – not man, but Jesus speaks – "Only believe" – in other words, "only trust." What is faith, but trust? what is believing in Jesus, but trusting in Jesus? When Jesus says, "only believe me," He literally says, "only trust me." And what a natural, beautiful, soothing definition of the word faith is this!

Many a volume has been written to explain the nature and illustrate the operation of faith – the subject and the reader remaining as much mystified and perplexed as ever. But who can fail to comprehend the meaning of the good old Saxon word trust! All can understand what this means. When, therefore, Jesus says – as He does to every individual who reads these words — "only believe me," He literally says, "only trust me." Thus He spoke to the anxious father who besought Him to come and heal his child: "only believe – only trust my power, only trust my compassion, only trust my word; do not be afraid, only trust me." And thus He speaks to you, believer. Oh, for a heart to respond, "Speak, Lord, for your servant hears!"[1]

Trust implies, on our part, mystery and ignorance, danger and helplessness. How wrapped in inscrutability, how shadowy and unreal, is all the future! As we attempt to penetrate the dark clouds, what strange forebodings steal over our spirits. Just at this juncture Jesus approaches, and with address most winning, and in accents most gentle, speaks these words, "Only believe – only trust me! Trust me, who knows the end from the beginning;[2] trust me, who has all resources at my command;[3] trust me, whose love never changes, whose wisdom never misleads, whose word never fails,[4] whose eye never slumbers nor sleeps[5] – only trust me!" Enough, my blessed Lord, my soul replies. I will sit myself down a loving child, a lowly disciple at Your feet, and, indistinct and dreary as my future path may be, will learn from You how and where I may trust You all my journey through. (Winslow, Morning Thoughts, p. Jul 16)

Footnotes:
1. 1 Samuel 3:9-10.
2. Isaiah 46:10.
3. John 3:35; John 13:3; 2 Peter 1:3; Matthew 28:18-20.
4. Isaiah 55:11.
5. Psalm 121:3-4.

33

Reading: Matthew 8:14-34

"*When evening came, they brought to him many who were demon-possessed. He drove out the spirits with a word and healed all who were sick, so that what was spoken through the prophet Isaiah might be fulfilled: He himself took our weaknesses and carried our diseases."*
Matthew 8:16-17

In one respect only may it be said, that our Divine and adorable Lord would seem to have been exempted from the physical infirmities' peculiar to the nature which He so voluntarily and entirely assumed – it does not appear that He was ever, in His own person, the subject of sickness or disease. It is indeed declared by His inspired biographer, thus confirming at the same time a prediction of one of the prophets, "Himself took our infirmities, and bare our sicknesses;"[1] but this He did in the same manner in which He bore our moral sicknesses, without any personal participation. He bore our sins, but He was Himself sinless.[2] He carried our sicknesses, but He Himself was a stranger to disease. And His exemption from the one will explain His exemption from the other. His humanity knew no sin; it was that "holy thing" begotten by the Holy Spirit, and as stainless as God Himself. As sin introduced into our nature every kind of physical evil, and disease among the rest, our Lord's freedom from the cause necessarily left Him free from the effect. He was never sick, because He never sinned. No, He had never died, had He not consented to die. With a nature prepared and conceived totally without moral taint, there were no seeds of decay from which death could reap its harvest. Under no sentence of dissolution, death had no power to claim Him as its victim. As pure as our first parents before the fall, like them in their original state of holiness, He was naturally deathless and immortal. Had He not, by an act of the most stupendous grace, taken upon Him the curse and sin of His Church, thereby making Himself responsible to Divine justice for the utmost payment of her debt, the "bitterness of death" had never touched His lips. But even then His death was voluntary. His relinquishment of life was His own act and deed. The Jew who hunted Him to the cross, and the Roman by whose hands He died, were but the actors in the awful tragedy. The "king of terrors" wrenched not His spirit from Him. Death waited the permission of Essential Life before he winged the fatal dart. "Jesus yielded up the spirit,"[3] literally, made a surrender, or let go His spirit. Thus violent though it was, and responsible for the crime as were its agents, the death of Jesus was yet voluntary. "I lay down my life,"[4] are His expressive words.

The control and power of Christ over bodily disease form one of the most instructive and tender pages of His history when upon earth. We can but briefly refer the reader to a few of the different traits of the Divine Physician's grace, as illustrated by the various cures which He effected. His promptness in healing the nobleman's son,[5] His unsolicited cure of the sick man at the pool of Bethesda, and the man with a withered hand.[6] The humility and delicacy with which He heals the centurion's servant.[7] The tenderness with which He restored the widow's son.[8] The simplicity with which He recovered the man born blind.[9] The gentle touch with which He cured the man, sick of the dropsy.[10] The natural and spiritual healing of the paralytic.[11] The resistless compassion with which He cured the daughter of the Syrophoenician woman.[12] The wisdom and the authority with which He healed the lunatic child.[13] The power with which He ejected the demons from the man, permitting their entrance into the swine.[14] Truly the name of our Divine Physician is "Wonderful!"[15] All this skill and power and feeling He still possesses; and in their exercise, in His present dealings with His suffering saints, is He glorified. (Winslow, Evening Thoughts, p. Apr 20)

Footnotes:
1. Isaiah 53.
2. Hebrews 4:15.
3. Matthew 27:50.
4. John 10:18.
5. John 4:43-54.
6. John 5:1-9; Mark 3:1-6.
7. Matthew 8:5-13.
8. Luke 7:11-17.
9. John 9:1-7.
10. Luke 14:1-6.
11. Luke 5:17-28.
12. Mark 8:24-30.
13. Luke 9:37-43.
14. Matthew 8:28-34.
15. Isaiah 9:6.

34

Reading: Matthew 9

"... the Son of Man has authority on earth to forgive sins ..."
Matthew 9:6

Behold one of the great Physician's mightiest arts: he has power to forgive sin! While here he lived below, before the ransom had been paid, before the blood had been literally sprinkled on the mercy-seat, he had power to forgive sin. Hath he not power to do it now that he hath died? What power must dwell in him who to the utmost farthing has faithfully discharged the debts of his people! He has boundless power now that he has finished transgression and made an end of sin.[1] If ye doubt it, see him rising from the dead! behold him in ascending splendor raised to the right hand of God! Hear him pleading before the eternal Father, pointing to his wounds, urging the merit of his sacred passion! What power to forgive is here! "He hath ascended on high, and received gifts for men."[2] "He is exalted on high to give repentance and remission of sins."[3] The most crimson sins are removed by the crimson of his blood. At this moment, dear reader, whatever thy sinfulness, Christ has power to pardon, power to pardon thee, and millions such as thou art. A word will speak it. He has nothing more to do to win thy pardon; all the atoning work is done. He can, in answer to thy tears, forgive thy sins today, and make thee know it. He can breathe into thy soul at this very moment a peace with God which passeth all understanding, which shall spring from perfect remission of thy manifold iniquities. Dost thou believe that? I trust thou believest it. Mayst thou experience now the power of Jesus to forgive sin! Waste no time in applying to the Physician of souls, but hasten to him with words like these: —

> *"Jesus! Master! hear my cry;*
> *Save me, heal me with a word;*
> *Fainting at thy feet I lie,*
> *Thou my whisper'd plaint hast heard."*
> (Spurgeon, p. Evening Aug 10)

Footnotes:
1. Hebrews 9:26.
2. Psalm 68:18.
2. Acts 5:31.

35

Reading: Matthew 10

"...Matthew the Publican ..." Matthew 10:3 (AKJV)

It ought not to be overlooked, in the account of this apostle of Jesus, that in the list given by the other Evangelists, of our Lord's disciples, he is placed before Thomas;[1] but in this, of his own, he places Thomas first. And whereas, after his call to the apostleship, the brethren, in making mention of him, dropped his former occupation of a *publican,* yet Matthew himself still preserves it. Grace always humbles. The call of this man, the distinguishing nature of that grace, the effects and blessedness of it, open some sweet thoughts for meditation, which, under divine teaching, cannot fail of being profitable to the saint, and encouraging to the sinner: and it will be well, my soul, for thee to exercise thine evening devotion upon it. He was a *publican;* that is, a tax-gatherer for the Romans. Of such characters we cannot have a more lively idea, than from what our Lord himself said of them. For when Jesus, in his description of a sinner more than ordinarily to be avoided, sets him forth as such, he said, "Let him be to thee as an heathen man and a publican."[2] Such was Matthew when called. And where was he when called? Not in the synagogue, attending the means of grace, or desiring to seek the Lord; but when seeking him not, yea, sitting at the seat of custom, and fully engaged in his pursuit of worldly gain. Pause, my soul, and mark the property of grace! Surely in this man's instance, as well as in thousands of others, the Lord might say, "I am found of them that sought me not!"[3] And oh! what a surprising, unexpected, unlooked-for call, was that of the Lord Jesus to *Matthew!* What a powerful, gracious, saving, and effectual call was it! Precious Redeemer! are we not authorized to consider all these, and other similar points of view, as purposely intended to tell poor sinners, like Matthew, that thy grace is not the effect of our merit, nor the result of any man's worth? Surely, Lord, every poor sinner may from this learn, that whatever best tends to magnify the riches of thy grace, must be in the purposes of thy holy will and pleasure. Hence it is, that thou makest thy grace to shine on such lost, ruined, and undone sinners as we are. But, my soul, take another short view of this man, and thy Savior's grace towards him. When the Lord had called him by his grace, he invited the Lord to his home: no sooner did Jesus open Matthew's heart, than Matthew opened his house to receive Jesus. See to it, my soul, that thou art daily manifesting the same proofs of *thy* calling. Oh! for grace to take Jesus home to our hearts, to our houses, to our neighbors, to our families, children, and servants, if we have any, and spread forth the sweet savor of his name, and the efficacy of his blood and righteousness, in every direction. Like the psalmist, let our language be, "O come hither, and hearken, all ye that fear God: and I will tell you what he hath done for my soul!"[4] (Hawker, The Poor Man's Evening Portion, pp. 152–153)

Footnotes:
1. Mark 3:16-18; Luke 6:12-16.
2. Matthew 18:17.

3. Romans 10:20; Isaiah 65:1.
4. Psalm 66:16.

36

Reading: Mark 6

"... Come away by yourselves to a remote place and rest for a while ..."
Mark 6:31

Suffer me, dear reader, to urge upon you the daily and diligent cultivation of that Christianity which derives its freshness, its vigor, and its radiance, from much hidden communion with Jesus. We plead not for the religion of the recluse. A monkish Christianity is not the Christianity of the Bible. When God, in the exercise of His sovereign grace, converts a man, He converts him, not for himself only, but also for others. He converts him, not for the Church alone, but also for the world. He is to be a monument, whose inscription all may read – a city whose beauty all may admire – a burning and a shining light, in whose radiance all may rejoice. He is to live and labor, and, if need be, die for others. But we plead for more of that Christianity which is often alone with God: which withdraws at periods from the fatigue of labor and the din of strife, to renew its strength, and to replenish its resources, in a secret waiting upon the Lord. Christians must be more alone with Jesus. In the midst of what a whirlpool of excitement and of turmoil do numbers live!

How few withdraw from domestic and public enjoyments – the calls of business, the duties of committees, of secretaryships, and of agencies – to hold communion alone with God! This must not be. The institutions which they serve, the calling at which they toil, the families for whom they labor, would be the gainers, rather than the losers, by their occasional sequesterment from the world, to be alone with God. And were our Lord still upon the earth, contemplating their incessant action, their little devotional retirement, and consequent leanness of spirit, would He not be constrained to address them as He once tenderly did His jaded and exhausted disciples, "Come you yourselves apart into a desert place, and rest awhile." He would allure them from others to Himself. Do not be surprised at any way which the Lord may take to bring your weary soul to rest in Himself. It is not always in the crowd that He speaks most tenderly to the heart. More frequently He leads His people out, and takes them apart by Himself alone. It is often in the privacy of separation and retirement, when the soul is curtained within his pavilion, that the greatest and the sweetest nearness to Jesus are experienced. "Behold, I will allure her into the wilderness, and speak comfortably to her,"[1] – (margin, speak friendly to her heart). Has the Lord been leading you about – severing this tie, and breaking up that repose; disappointing you here, and thwarting you there? Amazed, you have asked, "Lord, why this?" And the only reply has been the comfort which He has spoken to your weary, desolate heart. Thus does He make good in your experience His own exceeding great and precious promise – "I have satiated the weary soul, and I have replenished every sorrowful soul."[2] (Winslow, Evening Thoughts, p. Mar 30)

Footnotes:
1. Hosea 2:14.
2. Jeremiah 31:25.

37

Reading: Luke 9:1-17

"Summoning the Twelve, he gave them power and authority over all the demons and to heal diseases. Then he sent them to proclaim the kingdom of God and to heal the sick." Luke 9:1-2

The two former Evangelists have given us an account of our Lord's ordination of his apostles; Matthew 10:1, and Mark 3:14, 6:7; and there is somewhat truly interesting in the relation of it. But certainly, the commission, at this time, must have been very limited. For the apostles themselves, had but imperfect notions of their Lord's kingdom of grace, leading to his kingdom of glory. So strongly were their minds rivetted in the Jewish nation of a temporal kingdom, that not even the death of Christ had power to do away the impression. See, in proof, Acts 1:6, 8. (Hawker, Poor Man's New Testament Commentary: Matthew-John, p. 393)

38

Reading: Matthew 14

"O thou of little faith, wherefore didst thou doubt?" Matthew 14:31 (AKJV)

My soul! how sweet is it to eye Jesus in all things, and to be humbled in the recollection of his compassions to thy unaccountable instances of unbelief, after the many, nay continued, and daily experiences which thou hast had of his love and faithfulness. And doth thy Jesus speak to thee this day, in those expostulating words, "Oh thou of little faith, wherefore didst thou doubt?" What answer wilt thou return? Is there anything in thy life to justify, or even to apologize, for doubting? Look back – Behold thy God and Father's grace, and mercy, and love! A Savior so rich, so compassionate, so answering all wants, in spirituals, temporals, and eternals! A blessed Spirit, so condescending to teach,[1] to lead, and by his influences, to be continually with thee! Surely a life like thine, crowded with mercies, blessings upon blessings, and one miracle of grace followed by another – wherefore shouldest thou doubt? What shall I say to thee, oh thou that art the hope of Israel, and the Savior thereof! Lord give me to believe, and help thou mine unbelief. I beseech thee, my

God and Savior, give me henceforth faith to trust thee when I cannot trace thee: give me to hang upon thee when the ground of all sensible comforts seems sinking under my feet. I would cling to the faithfulness of my God in Christ, and throw my poor arms around thee, thou blessed Jesus! when all things appear the most dark and discouraging. And thus, day by day, living a life of faith and whole dependence upon thy glorious Person and thy glorious work, pressing after more sensible communion with thee, and more imparted strength and grace from thee, until at length, when thou shalt call me home from a life of faith to a life of sight – then, precious Jesus! would I say to thee, with my dying breath, "Oh present me, washed in thy blood and clothed in thy righteousness, among the whole body of thy glorious church, not having spot or wrinkle, or any such thing, but that I may be without blame before thee in love."[2] (Hawker, The Poor Man's Morning Portion, p. Mar 13)

Footnotes:
1. John 14:26.
2. Ephesians 5:27.

39

Reading: John 6

"For him hath God the Father sealed." John 6:27 (AKJV)

My soul! hast thou ever remarked the peculiar glory of those scriptures which take within a small compass the whole persons of the Godhead, as concurring and co-operating in the grand business of salvation? No doubt, all scripture is blessed, being given by inspiration of God;[1] but there is a peculiar blessedness in these sweet portions, which, at one view, represent the Holy Three in One unitedly engaged in the sinner's redemption. My soul! ponder over this divine passage in thy Savior's discourse, as thus: Who is the *him*, here spoken of, but the Lord Jesus? And whom but God the Father could seal Christ? And with whom was Christ sealed and anointed, but by God the Holy Spirit? Would anyone have thought, at first view, that in *seven words*, such a blessed testimony should be given to the glorious foundation-truth of the whole Bible? "For him hath God the Father sealed." Precious Jesus! enable me to behold thy divine authority as the warrant for faith, in this gracious act of thy Father. And while I view thee as infinitely suited for my poor soul, in every state, and under every circumstance, let my soul find confidence in the conviction that the validity of all thy gracious acts of salvation is founded in the seal of the Spirit.[2] Yes! thou dear Lord, it was indeed Jehovah the Spirit that was upon thee, when thou wast anointed "to preach the gospel to the poor, to heal the broken in heart, to give deliverance to the captive, and the restoring of sight to the blind, to set at liberty them that are bruised, and to proclaim the acceptable year of the Lord."[3] And art thou, dearest Lord, thus held forth, and thus recommended, by the grand seal of heaven, to every poor sinner who feels a conscious want of salvation? Oh, then, help, Lord, by thy blessed Spirit, all and every one of this description, so to receive a sealed Savior, as to rest in nothing short of being sealed by him; and while every act of love, and every tendency of grace, proclaims thee, blessed Jesus, as "him whom God the Father hath sealed," so let every act of faith, and every tendency of the soul, in the goings forth after thee, be expressive of the same earnest longings as the Church, of being sealed and owned by thee, when she cried out: "Set me as a seal upon thy heart, as a seal upon thine arm: for love is strong as death: jealousy is cruel as the grave: the coals thereof are coals of fire, which hath a most vehement flame."[4] (Hawker, The Poor Man's Evening Portion, p. Apr 3)

Footnotes:
1. 2 Timothy 3:16.
2. 2 Corinthians 1:21-23; Ephesians 4:30.
3. Luke 4:17-19.
4. Song of Songs / Solomon 8:6.

40

Reading: Mark 7

"Summoning the crowd again..." Mark 7:14

I admire this discourse of the Lord Jesus to the people. And I cannot but admire it the more, because from the distinguishing manner in which it is said *he called them,* and introduced what he said to them, in charging them to hear that there were many of them his people, in contradistinction to the Pharisees around. And I cannot from hence help requesting the Reader to remark with me, how uniformly this distinction hath been preserved in the Church of Christ, in reading or preaching the word, from that time to the present hour. When we see (as that we cannot but see) in every congregation, *some* receiving the word with holy joy of the Holy Spirit, as *Paul* testified the Church of the *Thessalonians* did: whilst *others,* like those *Pharisees,* seeking only to find fault; what can be more decisive in testimony to the same. And though many, like those *Pharisees,* are, as far as outward appearances go, apparently decent and moral in their lives and conversation with men; and others, in the religion of nature, seem to act up to the principles of external godliness, as high as natural strength can reach; yea, some of them make a profession of the Gospel, and are ready to compliment Christ to make up their deficiency; yet, in all these there is not an atom of regenerating grace; it is the old tang of the old nature, neither are they any of them savingly acquainted with the person, work, grace, and glory, of the Lord Jesus Christ. If the Reader wishes to have a true scriptural account of the real saving work of God the Holy Spirit upon the heart, I refer him to the picture drawn by inspiration in the first Chapter of Paul's first Epistle to the Thessalonians. In verse the 4th, the Apostle states the knowledge of election. In the 5th, he shews how it was proved and made known. In verse the 6th, he shews the sure effects of it in themselves. And in the four verses which follow, he shews the evidences which were proved thereby to others. (Hawker, Poor Man's New Testament Commentary: Matthew-John, pp. 250–251)

41

Reading: Matthew 15

"And she said, Truth, Lord: yet the dogs eat of the crumbs which fall from their master's table." Matthew 15:27

This woman gained comfort in her misery by thinking GREAT THOUGHTS OF CHRIST. The Master had talked about the children's bread: "Now," argued she, "since thou art the Master of the table of grace, I know that thou art a generous housekeeper, and there is sure to be abundance of bread on thy table; there will be such an abundance for the children that there will be crumbs to throw on the floor for the dogs, and the children will fare none the worse because the dogs are fed." She thought him one who kept so good a table that all that she needed would only be a crumb in comparison; yet remember, what she wanted was to have the devil cast out of her daughter. It was a very great thing to her, but she had such a high esteem of Christ, that she said, "It is nothing to him, it is but a crumb for Christ to give." This is the royal road to comfort. Great thoughts of your sin alone will drive you to despair; but great thoughts of Christ will pilot you into the haven of peace. "My sins are many, but oh! it is nothing to Jesus to take them all away. The weight of my guilt presses me down as a giant's foot would crush a worm, but it is no more than a grain of dust to him, because he has already borne its curse in his own body on the tree. It will be but a small thing for him to give me full remission, although it will be an infinite blessing for me to receive it." The woman opens her soul's mouth very wide, expecting great things of Jesus, and he fills it with his love. Dear reader, do the same. She confessed what Christ laid at her door, but she laid fast hold upon him, and drew arguments even out of his hard words; she believed great things of him, and she thus overcame him. SHE WON THE VICTORY BY BELIEVING IN HIM. Her case is an instance of prevailing faith; and if we would conquer like her, we must imitate her tactics. (Spurgeon, p. Evening Mar 27)

42

Reading: Mark 8

"When he cometh in the glory of his Father with the holy angels."
Mark 8:38

If we have been partakers with Jesus in his shame, we shall be sharers with him in the luster which shall surround him when he appears again in glory. Art thou, beloved one, with Christ Jesus? Does a vital union knit thee to him? Then thou art today with him in his shame; thou hast taken up his cross, and gone with him without the camp bearing his reproach; thou shalt doubtless be with him when the cross is exchanged for the crown. But judge thyself this evening; for if thou art not with him in the regeneration, neither shalt thou be with him when he shall come in his glory. If thou start back from the black side of communion, thou shalt not understand its bright, its happy period, when the King shall come, and all his holy angels with him. What! are angels with him? And yet he took not up angels – he took up the seed of Abraham. Are the holy angels with him? Come, my soul, if thou art indeed his own beloved, thou canst not be far from him. If his friends and his neighbors are called together to see his glory, what thinkest thou if thou art married to him? Shalt thou be distant? Though it be a day of judgment, yet thou canst not be far from that heart which, having admitted angels into intimacy, has admitted thee into union. Has he not said to thee, O my soul, "I will betroth thee unto me in righteousness, and in judgment, and in lovingkindness?"[1] Have not his own lips said it, "I am married unto thee, and my delight is in thee?"[2] If the angels, who are but friends and neighbors, shall be with him, it is abundantly certain that his own beloved Hephzibah, in whom is all his delight, shall be near to him, and sit at his right hand. Here is a morning star of hope for thee, of such exceeding brilliance, that it may well light up the darkest and most desolate experience. (Spurgeon, p. Evening Mar 26)

Footnotes:
1. Hosea 2:19.
2. Isaiah 62:4.

43

Reading: Luke 9:18-27

"Then he said to them all, "If anyone wants to follow after me, let him deny himself, take up his cross daily, and follow me. For whoever wants to save his life will lose it, but whoever loses his life because of me will save it." Luke 9:23-24

The life of our adorable Lord was a life of continuous trial. From the moment He entered our world He became leagued with suffering; He identified Himself with it in its almost endless forms. He seemed to have been born with a tear in His eye, with a shade of sadness on His brow. He was prophesied as "a man of sorrows and acquainted with grief."[1] And, from the moment He touched the horizon of our earth, from that moment His sufferings commenced. Not a smile lighted up His benign countenance from the time of His advent to His departure. He came not to indulge in a life of tranquility and repose; He came not to quaff the cup of earthly or of Divine sweets – for even this last was denied Him in the hour of His lingering agony on the cross. He came to suffer – He came to bear the curse – He came to drain the deep cup of wrath, to weep, to bleed, to die. Our Savior was a cross-bearing Savior: our Lord was a suffering Lord. And was it to be expected that they who had linked their destinies with His, who had avowed themselves His disciples and followers, should walk in a path diverse from their Lord's? He Himself speaks of the incongruity of such a division of interests: "The disciple is not above his Master, nor the servant above his Lord. It is enough for the disciple that he be as his Master, and the servant as his Lord."[2] There can be no true following of Christ as our example, if we lose sight of Him as a suffering Christ – a cross-bearing Savior. There must be fellowship with Him in His sufferings. In order to enter fully and sympathetically into the afflictions of His people, He stooped to a body of suffering: in like manner, in order to have sympathy with Christ in His sorrows, we must, in some degree tread the path He trod. Here is one reason why He ordained that along this rugged path His saints should all journey. They must be like their Lord; they are one with Him: and this oneness can only exist where there is mutual sympathy. The church must be a cross-bearing church; it must be an afflicted church. Its great and glorious Head sought not, and found not, repose here: this was not His rest. He turned His back upon the pleasures, the riches, the luxuries, and even the common comforts of this world, preferring a life of obscurity, penury, and suffering. His very submission seemed to impart dignity to suffering, elevation to poverty, and to invest with an air of holy sanctity a life of obscurity, need, and trial.

We have seen, then, that our blessed Lord sanctified, by His own submission, a life of suffering; and that all His followers, if they would resemble Him, must have fellowship with Him in His sufferings. The apostle Paul seems to regard this in the light of a privilege. "For unto you," he says, "it is given in behalf of Christ, not only to believe on Him, but also to suffer for His sake."[3] It seems, too, to be regarded as a part of their calling. "For even hereunto were you called: because Christ also suffered for us, leaving us an example, that you should follow His steps."[4] Happy will be that afflicted child of God, who is led to view his Father's discipline in the light of a privilege. To drink of the cup that Christ drank of – to bear any part of the cross that He bore – to tread in any measure the path that He trod, is a privilege indeed. This is a distinction which angels have never attained. They know not the honor of suffering with Christ, of being made conformable to His death. It is peculiar to the believer in Jesus – it is his privilege, his calling. (Winslow, Evening Thoughts, p. Sep 25)

Footnotes:
1. Isaiah 53:3.
2. Matthew 10:24.
3. Philippians 1:29.
4. 1 Peter 2:21.

44

Reading: Matthew 16

"From then on Jesus began to point out to his disciples that it was necessary for him to go to Jerusalem and suffer many things..." Matthew 16:21

Observe with what tenderness the Lord Jesus begins to prepare the minds of his disciples for the great event coming. Oh! the love of Jesus! But observe the mistaken views of *Peter* upon the occasion. No doubt it was love in Peter to the person of his Lord, which could not bear the thought of his dear Lord's sufferings. But alas! *Peter* what would have become of Christ's Church, if Jesus had not died to redeem it? I have often paused over the passage. Think what Christ said to his dear servant; *get thee behind me Satan!*[1] Is this *Peter*, who, but a little before, Jesus, the Son of God, declared to be blessed? Never did the Lord Jesus use such language, and that to a child of God, and one of his own redeemed ones. But, Reader! while you and I consider, as in the instance of *Peter*, how a soul may be made blessed in the abundance of revelations, yet what temptations the same may fall into, when the Lord remits but a moment his teachings: and while we learn this from the character of this Apostle, let us yet abundantly more look unto the Lord Jesus in this instance, and see how his zeal for his Father's glory, and an holy love to his body, the Church, made him long for the hour, when, by his sufferings and death, he should accomplish redemption for his people. Oh! thou precious Lord Jesus! with what earnestness didst thou enter on this baptism of sufferings, and how wast thou straitened until it was accomplished! (Hawker, Poor Man's New Testament Commentary: Matthew-John, p. 115)

Footnote:
1. Matthew 16:23.

45

Reading: Mark 9

"The people, when they beheld him, were greatly amazed, and running to him saluted him." Mark 9:15

How great the difference between Moses and Jesus! When the prophet of Horeb had been forty days upon the mountain, he underwent a kind of transfiguration, so that his countenance shone with exceeding brightness, and he put a veil over his face, for the people could not endure to look upon his glory.[1] Not so our Savior. He had been transfigured with a greater glory than that of Moses, and yet, it is not written that the people were blinded by the blaze of his countenance, but rather they were amazed, and running to him they saluted him. The glory of the law repels, but the greater glory of Jesus attracts. Though Jesus is holy and just, yet blended with his purity there is so much of truth and grace,[2] that sinners run to him amazed at his goodness, fascinated by his love; they salute him, become his disciples, and take him to be their Lord and Master. Reader, it may be that just now you are blinded by the dazzling brightness of the law of God. You feel its claims on your conscience, but you cannot keep it in your life. Not that you find fault with the law, on the contrary, it commands your profoundest esteem, still you are in nowise drawn by it to God; you are rather hardened in heart, and are verging towards desperation. Ah, poor heart! turn thine eye from Moses, with all his repelling splendor, and look to Jesus, resplendent with milder glories. Behold his flowing wounds and thorn-crowned head! He is the Son of God, and therein he is greater than Moses, but he is the Lord of love, and therein more tender than the lawgiver. He bore the wrath of God, and in his death revealed more of God's justice than Sinai on a blaze, but that justice is now vindicated, and henceforth it is the guardian of believers in Jesus. Look, sinner, to the bleeding Savior, and as thou feelest the attraction of his love, fly to his arms, and thou shalt be saved. (Spurgeon, p. Evening Aug 26)

Footnotes:
1. Exodus 34:29-34.
2. John 1:14.

46

Reading: Luke 9:28-62

"... They became afraid as they entered the cloud." Luke 9:34

My soul! here is much instruction for thine evening thoughts to be employed upon. Sit down, and take a leisurely view of the situation of the disciples of Jesus at this hallowed season, on the mount. The Lord Jesus was about to manifest to them somewhat of his glory. But the prelude to it was infinitely solemn. "They feared as they entered into the cloud;" though, when there, Jesus was going to open to their souls the richest enjoyment of himself. And is it not so with all the sweetest manifestations which the Lord makes to his people? Seasons of sickness, bereaving providences, afflictions from the world, disappointments, crosses, and the like; these are like the cloud to the disciples, as we enter them; but what gracious events have we found folded up in them, and when opened to our view, how much of Jesus's love, and grace, and glory, have come out of them, which, but for the dispensation, we must have lost. And recollect, my soul, as thou lookest back, and tracest the divine hand leading thee through dark and trying providences, in how many cases, and in how many instances, though the cloud was frowning as thou didst enter, the most blessed sunshine soon after broke in upon thee. Precious Jesus! choose for me in every circumstance yet remaining to be accomplished. I know not what is in thy sovereign appointments concerning me; but sure I am, that both love and wisdom are at the bottom of all. Give me grace to enter the cloud, be it what it may, without fear, because I know Jesus is with me: and though, in this my day, it be neither clear nor dark, yet well I know all shall be well in thee, and from thee; "and at evening time it shall be light."[1] (Hawker, The Poor Man's Evening Portion, p. 316)

Footnote:
1. Zechariah 14:7.

47

Reading: Matthew 17

"When the disciples heard this, they fell facedown and were terrified." Matthew 17:6

It is not to be wondered at that the disciples should be thus affected. God is awful, even in mercies. See how Israel was struck with fear on *Mount Sinai.*[1] But see, Reader, the tenderness of Jesus. *He came and touched them,* Precious Redeemer! how hast thou, by the assumption of our nature, opened a way of communicating mercies to us, and lessening our fears. And Reader! I pray you to remark, that the very first words Jesus spake to his disciples after God the Father had commanded them to hear him, was, *be not afraid.* And doth it not follow, from hence, that such is the love of God our Father to the Church, in Christ, and knowing that all love is in the heart of Christ towards his people, thus he commands concerning him. And God the Son, having taking our nature for the express purpose, manifests that his whole heart towards them is love. And God the Holy Spirit, from his everlasting love also to Christ, and his Church in him, takes care to make the whole effectual, in *directing the heart of the redeemed into the love of God, and into the patient waiting for Jesus Christ!* Oh! for grace, under those blessed assurances, to possess such faith in Jesus, as may raise our souls above all fears, while conscious of a union with Christ, and acceptance in Christ. The sudden departure, of *Moses* and *Elias* may serve to teach us, that none but Jesus can be our abiding comfort. Everything here below is short and transitory. Oh! what a blessed thought it is. Jesus hath said, *Lo! I am with you always.*[2] (Hawker, Poor Man's New Testament Commentary: Matthew-John, pp. 119–120)

Footnotes:
1. Exodus 20:18–21.
2. Matthew 28:20.

48

Reading: Matthew 18

"Then Peter approached him and asked, "Lord, how many times shall I forgive my brother or sister who sins against me? As many as seven times?" "I tell you, not as many as seven," Jesus replied, "but seventy times seven.""" Matthew 18:21-22

If there is a single exercise of divine grace in which, more than in any other, the believer resembles God, it is this. God's love to man is exhibited in one great and glorious manifestation, and a single word expresses it – forgiveness. In nothing has He so gloriously revealed Himself as in the exercise of this divine prerogative. Nowhere does He appear so like Himself as here. He forgives sin, and the pardon of sin involves the bestowment of every other blessing. How often are believers called upon thus to imitate God! And how like him in spirit, in affection, and in action do they appear, when, with true greatness of soul and with lofty magnanimity of mind, they fling from their hearts, and efface from their memories, all traces of the offence that has been given, and of the injury that has been received! How affecting and illustrious the example of the expiring Redeemer! At the moment that His deepest wound was inflicted, as if blotting out the sin and its remembrance with the very blood that it shed, He prayed, as the last drop fell, and as the last breath departed, "Father, forgive them."[1] How fully and fearfully might He have avenged Himself at that moment! A stronger than Samson hung upon the cross. And as He bowed His human nature and gave up the spirit, He could as easily have bowed the pillars of the universe, burying His murderers beneath its ruins. But no! He was too great for this. His strength should be on the side of mercy. His revenge should wreak itself in compassion. He would heap coals of fire upon their heads. He would overcome and conquer their evil, but He would overcome and conquer it with good: "Father, forgive them."

It is in the constant view of this forgiveness that the followers of Christ desire, on all occasions of offence given, whether real or imaginary, to "forgive those who trespass against them."[2] Themselves the subjects of a greater and diviner forgiveness, they would be prompt to exercise the same holy feeling towards an offending brother. In the remembrance of the ten thousand talents from whose payment his Lord has released him, he will not hesitate to cancel the hundred pence owing to him by his fellow-servant. Where, then, will you find any exercise of brotherly love more God-like and divine than this? In its immediate tender, its greatest sweetness and richest charm appear. The longer it is delayed, the more difficult becomes the duty. The imagination is allowed to dwell upon, and the mind to brood over, a slight offence received, perhaps never intended, until it has increased to such magnitude as almost to extend, in the eye of the aggrieved party, beyond the limit of forgiveness. And then follows an endless train of evils – the wound festers and inflames; the breach widens; coldness is manifested; malice is cherished; every word, look, and act is misinterpreted; the molehill grows into a mountain, the little rivulet swells into an ocean, until happiness and peace retire from scenes so uncongenial, and from hearts so full of all hatred and strife. But how lovely in its appearance, and how pleasurable in the feelings it enkindles, is a prompt exercise of Christian forgiveness! Before the imagination has had time to distort, or the wound to fester, or ill-minded people to interfere, Christian love has triumphed, and all is forgiven!

How full of meaning is our blessed Lord's teaching on this point of Christian duty, in our motto! It behooves us prayerfully and constantly to ponder His word. True love has no limits to its forgiveness. If it observes in the bosom of the offender the faintest marks of regret, of contrition, and of return, like Him from whose heart it comes, it is "ready to forgive," even "until seventy times seven." Oh who can tell the debt we owe to His repeated, perpetual forgiveness? And shall I refuse to be reconciled to my brother? Shall I withhold from him the hand of love, and let the sun go down upon my wrath? Because he has trampled upon me, who have so often acknowledged myself the chief of sinners, because he has slighted my self-importance, or has wounded my pride, or has grieved my too sensitive spirit, or, it is possible, without just cause, has uttered hard speeches, and has lifted up his heel against me, shall I keep alive the embers of an unforgiving spirit in my heart? Or rather, shall I heap coals of fire upon his head,[3] not to consume him with wrath, but to overcome him with love? How has God my Father, how has Jesus my Redeemer, my Friend, dealt with me? Even so will I deal with my offending brother. I will not even wait until he comes, and acknowledges his fault. I will go to him, and tell him that at the mercy-seat, beneath the cross, with my eye upon the loving, forgiving heart of God, I have resolved to forgive all, and will forget all. (Winslow, Evening Thoughts, p. Jun 23)

Footnotes:
1. Luke 23:34.

2. Matthew 6:12.
3. Proverbs 25:22.

49

Reading: John 7

"Never man spake like this man." John 7:46 (AKJV)

What a decided testimony were even the enemies of Christ compelled, from their own consciences, to give to the Godhead and power of the Lord Jesus Christ! Think then, my soul, what an evidence thou wouldst bring, if called upon to tell what Jesus hath said to thee! From the first moment that Jesus revealed himself *in* his word, and *by* his word, to thy heart, thou couldst truly say, as the Jewish officers did, "Never man spake like this man." Never any spake like this God-man this Glory-man, thy Redeemer. All his words were, and are, divine words; powerful, persuasive, tender, gracious words, and full of salvation. Say how very blessed all that Jesus spake of salvation was to thy heart, when he made it personal and spake it all to *thee*. When he said, I am *thy* salvation. I have pardon, I have peace, I have righteousness, I have grace here, and glory hereafter; and all I have is for *thee*. So that when reading the word, or hearing the word, and the question arose in thy heart, To whom speaketh my Lord thus? oh, how unspeakably precious did the word become, when Jesus said by his servant, "To you is the word of this salvation sent."[1] Precious Lord Jesus! how shall I express my soul's sense of thy love and grace, thy mercy and favor? Since thou first manifested thyself to my heart, I am no longer my own. Thou hast taken all my affections with thee to heaven, and caused them to center everything in thyself. And now, Lord, I still daily, yea sometimes hourly, when I hear thy voice, am constrained to cry out "Never man spake like this man!" How sweet and suitable are thy words to my weary soul; thou hast indeed "the tongue of the learned, and knowest how to speak in season to souls," like mine, "that are weary."[2] How truly blessed and seasonable is thy well-known voice to my soul, when a sense of my nothingness makes thy fulness yet more precious. Oh! when I hear thee say, "My grace is sufficient for thee, for my strength is made perfect in weakness," surely, Lord, I feel a power that makes all my enemies seem as nothing. Like thy servant, I then truly "glory in my infirmities, that thy power may rest upon thee."[3] Be thou, then, dearest Lord Jesus, all I need, and let me hear thy voice, and see thy countenance; for, both in life and in death, in time and to all eternity, the voice of my Lord Jesus will be my everlasting comfort, for none speaketh like thee! (Hawker, The Poor Man's Evening Portion, pp. 244–245)

Footnotes:
1. Acts 13:26.
2. Isaiah 50:4.
3. 2 Corinthians 12:9-10.

50

Reading: John 8

"*Go, and sin no more.*" John 8:11 (AKJV)

See how Christ manifests His abhorrence of the sin, while He throws His shield of mercy around the sinner. The Lord does not justify the sinner's transgression, though He justifies the sinner's person. In the great matter of salvation, justification and sanctification, pardon and holiness, are essentially and inseparably united. When the Lord Jesus dismisses a sinner with a sense of acquittal in his conscience, it is ever accompanied with that most affecting of all exhortations, "Sin no more." And as he passes out from the presence of Jesus, pardoned, justified, saved, the Savior's tender, soul-subduing words from that moment seem to vibrate upon his ear every step of his onward way. "Go, admire, and publish abroad the glory of that grace that has done such great things for you. Go, and spread His fame, and with your latest breath dwell upon His name, who, when sin and Satan and conscience accused you, and would have consigned you to eternal woe – then appeared your Friend,[1] your Advocate,[2] and your Savior.[3] Go, and when tempted to wound afresh the bosom that sheltered you, remember Me; from

Gethsemane, from Calvary, and from the hallowed spot where I spoke to you, I condemn you not. Go, and sin no more." (Winslow, Morning Thoughts, p. Feb 26)

Footnotes:
1. John 15:15.
2. 1 John 2.
3. 2 Timothy 1:10.

51

Reading: John 9:1-10:21

"I am the door: by me if any man enter in, he shall be saved, and shall go in and out, and find pasture." John 10:9 (AKJV)

Jesus, the great I AM, is the entrance into the true church, and the way of access to God himself. He gives to the man who comes to God by him four choice privileges.

1. *He shall be saved.* The fugitive manslayer passed the gate of the city of refuge, and was safe.[1] Noah entered the door of the ark,[2] and was secure. None can be lost who take Jesus as the door of faith to their souls. Entrance through Jesus into peace is the guarantee of entrance by the same door into heaven. Jesus is the only door, an open door, a wide door, a safe door; and blessed is he who rests all his hope of admission to glory upon the crucified Redeemer.

2. *He shall go in.* He shall be privileged to go in among the divine family, sharing the children's bread, and participating in all their honors and enjoyments. He shall go in to the chambers of communion, to the banquets of love, to the treasures of

the covenant, to the storehouses of the promises. He shall go in unto the King of kings[3] in the power of the Holy Spirit, and the secret of the Lord shall be with him.
3. *He shall go out.* This blessing is much forgotten. We go out into the world to labor and suffer, but what a mercy to go in the name and power of Jesus! We are called to bear witness to the truth, to cheer the disconsolate, to warn the careless, to win souls, and to glorify God; and as the angel said to Gideon, "Go in this thy might,"[4] even thus the Lord would have us proceed as his messengers in his name and strength.
4. *He shall find pasture.* He who knows Jesus shall never want. Going in and out shall be alike helpful to him: in fellowship with God he shall grow, and in watering others he shall be watered. Having made Jesus his all, he shall find all in Jesus. His soul shall be as a watered garden, and as a well of water whose waters fail not.[5] (Spurgeon, p. Evening Dec 17)

Footnotes:
1. Numbers 35:9-29.
2. Genesis, chapter 7.
3. Revelation 17:14.
4. Judges 6:14.
5. Isaiah 58:11.

52

Reading: John 10:22-42

"My sheep hear my voice, I know them, and they follow me. I give them eternal life, and they will never perish. No one will snatch them out of my hand." John 10:27-28

As God-man Mediator, Christ is able to keep His people. As the covenant Head and Preserver of His Church, "it pleased the Father that in Him should all fullness dwell."[1] The Father knew what His beloved family would need. He knew what corruptions would threaten them, what temptations would beguile them, what foes would assail them, what infirmities would encompass them, and what trials would depress them; therefore it pleased Him, it was His own good and gracious pleasure, that in His Son, the Mediator of His beloved people, should all fullness dwell – a fullness of merit, a fullness of pardon, a fullness of righteousness, a fullness of grace, wisdom, and strength, commensurate with the varied, multiplied, and diversified circumstances of His family. It is "all fullness."

As the Mediator, then, of His people, He keeps them in perfect safety by night and by day. No man, no power, can pluck them out of His hands; He has undertaken their full salvation. To die for their sins, and to rise again for their justification, and yet not to provide for their security while traveling through a world of sin and temptation – to leave them to their own guardianship, an unprotected prey to their own heart's corruptions, the machinations of Satan, and the power of worldly entanglement – would have been but a partial salvation of His people. Opposed by a threefold enemy – Satan and the world in league with their own imperfectly renewed and sanctified hearts, that treacherous foe dwelling within the camp, ever ready to betray the soul into the hands of its enemies – how could a poor weak child of God bear up and breast this powerful phalanx? But He, who was mighty to save, is mighty to keep;[2] in Him provision is made for all the trying, intricate, perilous circumstances in which the believer may be placed. Grace is laid up for the subjection of every inbred corruption – an armor is provided for every assault of the foe; wisdom, strength, consolation, sympathy, kindness – all, all that a poor believing sinner can possibly require, is richly stored in Jesus, the covenant Head of all the fullness of God to His people.

But how is the child of God to avail himself of this provision? The simple but glorious life of faith exhibits itself here. By faith the believer travels up to this rich and ample supply; by faith he takes his nothingness to Christ's all-sufficiency; by faith he takes his unworthiness to Christ's infinite merit; by faith he takes his weakness to Christ's strength, his folly to Christ's wisdom; his fearful heart, his timid spirit, his nervous frame, his doubtful mind, his beclouded evidences, his rebellious will, his painful cross – his peculiar case, of whatever nature it may be – in the way of believing, in the exercise of simple faith, he goes with it to Jesus, and as an empty vessel hangs himself upon that "nail fastened in a sure place," the glorious Eliakim on whom is hung "all the glory of His Father's house, the offspring and the issue, all vessels of small quantity, from the vessels of cups even to all the vessels of flagons."[3] Thus may the weakest believer, the most severely assailed, the most deeply tried, the most painfully tempted, lay his Goliath dead at his feet, by a simple faith's dealing with the fullness that is in Christ Jesus. Oh, how mighty is the believer who, in deep distrust of his own power, casting off from him all spirit of self-dependence, looks simply and fully at Jesus, and goes forth to meet his enemy, only as he is "strong in the strength that is in Christ."[4] (Winslow, Morning Thoughts, p. Sep 3)

Footnotes:
1. Colossians 1:19.
2. 1 Peter 1:5.
3. Isaiah 22:23-24.
4. Ephesians 6:10.

53

Reading: Luke 10

"In that hour Jesus rejoiced in spirit." Luke 10:21 (AKJV)

The Savior was "a man of sorrows,"[1] but every thoughtful mind has discovered the fact that down deep in his innermost soul he carried an inexhaustible treasury of refined and heavenly joy. Of all the human race, there was never a man who had a deeper, purer, or more abiding peace than our Lord Jesus Christ. "He was anointed with the oil of gladness above his fellows."[2] His vast benevolence must, from the very nature of things, have afforded him the deepest possible delight, for benevolence is joy. There were a few remarkable seasons when this joy manifested itself. "At that hour Jesus rejoiced in spirit, and said, I thank thee, O Father, Lord of heaven and earth." Christ had his songs, though it was night with him; though his face was marred, and his countenance had lost the luster of earthly happiness, yet sometimes it was lit up with a matchless splendor of unparalleled satisfaction, as he thought upon the recompense of the reward, and in the midst of the congregation sang his praise unto God. In this, the Lord Jesus is a blessed picture of his church on earth. At this hour the church expects to walk in sympathy with her Lord along a thorny road; through much tribulation she is forcing her way to the crown. To bear the cross is her office, and to be scorned and counted an alien by her mother's children is her lot; and yet the church has a deep well of joy, of which none can drink but her own children.[2] There are stores of wine, and oil, and corn, hidden in the midst of our Jerusalem, upon which the saints of God are evermore sustained and nurtured; and sometimes, as in our Savior's case, we have our seasons of intense delight, for "There is a river, the streams whereof shall make glad the city of our God."[4] Exiles though we be, we rejoice in our King; yea, in him we exceedingly rejoice, while in his name we set up our banners. (Spurgeon, p. Evening Mar 24)

Footnotes:
1. Isaiah 53:3.
2. Psalm 45:7.
3. John 4:13; John 7:37.
4. Psalm 46:4.

54

Reading: Luke 11

Dearest Lord Jesus! I would say for myself, and all thy redeemed family, teach us to pray, and with what words to come before the Lord, in all our soul exercises, and wants, and conflicts, and trials. Do thou, dear Lord! by the sweet influences of thine Holy Spirit, both spread thy fullness, cause us to feel our need, excite a spiritual appetite, and open a constant source of communion, *that, from thy fullness, we may all receive and grace for grace!*[1] And oh! for a fervor in prayer, awakened by the Holy Spirit! that, like the friend at midnight, and *Jacob* at *Bethel*, never may we go to the mercy-seat, and come away empty; but, like the great father of the praying seed, in the same spirit of faith to tell our God, *I will not let thee go, except thou bless me.*[2] And, oh Lord! grant that neither the *Queen of the South, nor the Ninevites,* may bring reproach upon thy people! No Solomon like our Solomon – no preaching of *Jonah* like the preaching of our Lord Jesus Christ! Precious Master! let neither the awful state of *Pharisee* blindness, nor the wretched delusion of *Jewish* ignorance, be in the lot of thy redeemed, in all generations of thy Church. Oh!

for grace to sit at thy feet, to hear thy word! that through the blessed illumination of God the Holy Spirit, *our whole body,* as thou hast said, *being full of light, and having no part dark, the whole may be full of light!*[3] Jesus, the sun of righteousness,[4] shining *as when the bright shining of a candle doth give the people light.* (Hawker, Poor Man's New Testament Commentary: Matthew-John, pp. 416–417)

Footnotes:
1. John 1:16.
2. Genesis 32:26.
3. Luke 11:36.
4. Malachi 4:2.

55

Reading: Luke 12

"... and don't be anxious." Luke 12:29

My soul! it is a blessed thing to arrive at a fixed point, on the momentous concern of "the one thing needful."[1] As long as there remains any doubt or uncertainty whether Christ be the soul's portion or not, there is always a proportioned degree of doubt and uncertainty in the soul's comfort. What the dying patriarch said to his son, may with equal truth be said of every one of this description: "Unstable as water, thou shalt not excel."[2] For as long as the soul forms conclusions of safety, not from what Jesus is, but from what the soul's views of Jesus are, there will be always an unstable, unsettled state. And how many have I known, who are of doubtful mind whether they really do believe to the salvation of the soul, and yet have no doubt whether they be sinners, and both need and earnestly desire that salvation. They will tell you that Jesus is more precious than the golden wedge of *Ophir;* but they tell you, at the same time, they dare not say that they have an interest in his blood and righteousness. They see a loveliness in his person, and a suitableness to their necessities, in every point of view; but they cannot presume to hope that they do enjoy either. They can and do cry out, under the thirst of the soul, for Jesus, as David did for the waters of Bethlehem; but still, like David, they do not make use of the blessing, though it be procured them. My soul! it is blessed to live *above* doubts and fears, by living *upon* Jesus. The assurance of faith is founded in what Jesus is, and not what his people feel; in what view God the Father beholds Christ as the sinner's surety, and not what our apprehensions are concerning our present feelings. Faith is most strong where sense is most weak! and the glory given to Jesus is greater, when, like Abraham, "against hope, we believe in hope."[3] Blessed Lord Jesus! let the faith of my soul be the one fixed unalterable faith, that admits of no doubt nor change. Let me, with full purpose of heart, cleave unto the Lord. And while I can and do behold, through thy Spirit's teaching me, the Father's appointment and approbation, in all thy work and finished salvation: here let me fix, and never be of doubtful mind, but live and die in the full assurance of faith, well pleased with what my God and Father is well pleased with, and always "rejoicing in the hope of the glory of God!"[4] (Hawker, The Poor Man's Evening Portion, p. Oct 14)

Footnotes:
1. Luke 10:42.
2. Genesis 49:4.
3. Romans 4:18.
4. Romans 5:2.

56

Reading: Luke 13

"Sir, leave it this year also, until I dig around it and fertilize it. Perhaps it will produce fruit next year, but if not, you can cut it down."
Luke 13:8-9

Do I not behold the Lord Jesus here represented in his glorious office of our High-Priest and Intercessor?[1] And is it thus, that he so mercifully pleads for the unawakened and unprofitable among his people? Pause, my soul! Was it not from the effects of his intercession, that the world itself was spared from instant destruction, when Adam first broke through the fence of God's law? Is it not now by the same rich grace that thousands are spared from year to year *in* Christ Jesus, before that they are called to the knowledge *of* Christ Jesus? Nay, my soul! pause once more over the view of this wonderful subject, and ask thyself, Was it not from the same Almighty interposition that thou was kept from going down to the pit, during the long, long period of thy unregeneracy, while thou wert wholly unconscious of it? Hadst thou died in that unconverted state, where must have been thy portion? And was it from thy gracious intercession, blessed Jesus, that I then lived, that I am now spared, and, after all my barrenness, that another year of grace is opening before me? Oh precious, precious Jesus! suffer me to be no longer unfruitful in thy garden! Do, Lord, as thou hast said. Dig about me, and pour upon me all the sweet influences of thy Holy Spirit, which, like the rain, and the sun, and the dew of heaven, may cause me to bring forth fruit unto God. And, Lord! if so unworthy a creature may drop a petition at thy mercy-seat for others, let the coming year be productive of the same blessings to all thy redeemed; even to my poor unawakened relations; and to thousands of those who are yet in nature's darkness. Oh! that this may be to them the acceptable year of the Lord! (Hawker, The Poor Man's Morning Portion, p. Jan 2)

Footnote:
1. Hebrews 2:17; Hebrews 4:14-16; Romans 8:34.

57

Reading: Luke 14

"*Friend, go up higher.*" Luke 14:10 (AKJV)

When first the life of grace begins in the soul, we do indeed draw near to God, but it is with great fear and trembling. The soul conscious of guilt, and humbled thereby, is overawed with the solemnity of its position; it is cast to the earth by a sense of the grandeur of Jehovah, in whose presence it stands. With unfeigned bashfulness it takes the lowest room.

But, in after life, as the Christian grows in grace, although he will never forget the solemnity of his position, and will never lose that holy awe which must encompass a gracious man when he is in the presence of the God who can create or can destroy; yet his fear has all its terror taken out of it; it becomes a holy reverence, and no more an overshadowing dread. He is called up higher, to greater access to God in Christ Jesus. Then the man of God, walking amid the splendors of Deity, and veiling his face like the glorious cherubim, with those twin wings, the blood and righteousness of Jesus Christ, will, reverent and bowed in spirit, approach the throne; and seeing there a God of love, of goodness, and of mercy, he will realize rather the covenant character of God than his absolute Deity. He will see in God rather his goodness than his greatness, and more of his love than of his majesty. Then will the soul, bowing still as humbly as aforetime, enjoy a more sacred liberty of intercession; for while prostrate before the glory of the Infinite God, it will be sustained by the refreshing consciousness of being in the presence of boundless mercy and infinite love, and by the realization of acceptance "in the Beloved."[1] Thus the believer is bidden to come up higher, and is enabled to exercise the privilege of rejoicing in God, and drawing near to him in holy confidence, saying, "Abba, Father."[2]

"So may we go from strength to strength,
And daily grow in grace,
Till in thine image raised at length,
We see thee face to face."
(Spurgeon, p. Morning Dec 23)

Footnotes:
1. Ephesians 1:6.
2. Romans 8:15.

58

Reading: Luke 15

"Father, I have sinned." Luke 15:18

It is quite certain that those whom Christ has washed in his precious blood need not make a confession of sin, as culprits or criminals, before God the Judge, for Christ has for ever taken away all their sins in a legal sense, so that they no longer stand where they can be condemned, but are once for all accepted in the Beloved; but having become children, and offending as children, ought they not every day to go before their heavenly Father and confess their sin, and acknowledge their iniquity in that character?[1] Nature teaches that it is the duty of erring children to make a confession to their earthly father, and the grace of God in the heart teaches us that we, as Christians, owe the same duty to our heavenly Father. We daily offend, and ought not to rest without daily pardon. For, supposing that my trespasses against my Father are not at once taken to him to be washed away by the cleansing power of the Lord Jesus, what will be the consequence? If I have not sought forgiveness and been washed from these offences against my Father, I shall feel at a distance from him; I shall doubt his love to me; I shall tremble at him; I shall be afraid to pray to him: I shall grow like the prodigal, who, although still a child, was yet far off from his father. But if, with a child's sorrow at offending so gracious and loving a Parent, I go to him and tell him all, and rest not till I realize that I am forgiven, then I shall feel a holy love to my Father, and shall go through my Christian career, not only as saved, but as one enjoying present peace in God through Jesus Christ my Lord. There is a wide distinction between confessing sin *as a culprit*, and confessing sin as a child. The Father's bosom is the place for penitent confessions. We have been cleansed once for all, but our feet still need to be washed from the defilement of our daily walk as children of God.[2] (Spurgeon, p. Evening Feb 18)

Footnotes:
1. 1 John 1:9.
2. John 13:10.

59

Reading: Luke 16

"... How much do you owe my master? ..." Luke 16:5

My soul! if this question, which the unjust steward put to his lord's debtors, was put to thee, concerning that immense debt which hath made thee insolvent forever, what wouldest thou answer? Never couldst thou conceive the extent of it, much less think of paying the vast amount. A debtor to free grace for thy very *being;* a debtor to free grace for thy *well-being;* ten thousand talents, which the man in the parable owed his master, would not be sufficient to reckon up what thou in reality owest thy Lord, for even the common gifts of nature and of providence. But when the calculation goeth on in grace, what archangel shall write down the sum total? To the broken law of God, a bankrupt: exposed to the justice of God; to the dreadful penalty of everlasting death; to the fears and alarms of a guilty conscience; to the worm that dieth not; to the accusations of Satan, unable to answer one in a thousand. My soul, how much owest thou unto thy Lord? Are there yet any other outstanding debts? Oh! yes, infinitely and beyond all these. What thinkest thou, my soul, of Jesus? How much owest thou to the Father's love in giving, to the Redeemer's love in coming, and to the Holy Spirit in making the whole effectual to thy soul's joy; by which Jesus hath paid all thy debts, cancelled all the demands of God's righteous law, silenced Satan, answered justice; and not only redeemed thee out of the hands of everlasting bondage, misery, and eternal death, but brought thee into his everlasting kingdom of freedom, joy, and glory. Say, say, my soul, how much owest thou unto thy Lord? Oh, precious debt! ever increasing, and yet everlastingly making happy in owing. Lord Jesus, I am thine, and thy servant forever: thou hast loosed my bonds. (Hawker, The Poor Man's Morning Portion, p. Sep 24)

60

Reading: John 11

"Jesus wept." John 11:35

My soul! look at thy Redeemer in this account of him. Was there ever a more interesting portrait than what the evangelist hath here drawn of the Son of God? If the imagination were to be employed for ever in forming an interesting scene of the miseries of human nature, what could furnish so complete a picture, as these two words give of Christ, at the sight of them? "Jesus wept." Here we have at once the evidence how much the miseries of our nature affected the heart of Jesus; and here we have the most convincing testimony, that he partook of all the sinless infirmities of our nature, and was truly, and in all points, man as well as God. We are told by one of the ancient writers (as well as I recollect, it was *St. Chrysostom*) that some weak – but injudicious Christians, in his days, were so rash as to strike this verse out of their Bibles, from an idea, that it was unsuitable and unbecoming in the Son of God to weep. But we have cause to bless the overruling providence of God, that though they struck it out from their Bibles, they did it not from ours. It is blessed to us to have it preserved, for it affords one of the most delightful views we can possibly have of the affectionate heart of Jesus, in feeling for the sorrows of his people. And methinks, had they judged aright, they would have thought, that if it were unsuitable or unbecoming in Jesus to weep, it would have been more so to put on the appearance of it. And why those groans at the grave of Lazarus, if tears were improper? Precious Lord! How refreshing is to my soul, the consideration that "forasmuch as the children were partakers of flesh and blood, thou likewise didst take part of the same; that in all things it behooved thee to be made like to thy brethren!"[1] Hence, when my poor heart is afflicted; when Satan storms, or the world frowns; when sickness in myself, or when under bereaving providences for my friends, "all thy waves and storms seem to go over me;"[2] oh! what relief is it, to know that Jesus looks on, and sympathizes! Then do I say to myself, Will not Jesus, who wept at the grave of Lazarus, feel for me? Shall I look up to him, and look up in vain? Did Jesus, when upon earth, know what those exercises were; and was his precious soul made sensible of distresses, even to tears; and will he be regardless of what I feel, and the sorrows under which I groan? Oh, no! the sigh that bursts in secret from my heart, is not secret to him; the tear that on my night couch drops, unperceived and unknown to the world, is known and numbered by him. Though now exalted at the right hand of power, where he hath wiped away all tears from off all faces, yet he himself still retains the feelings and the character of "the man of sorrows, and of one well acquainted with grief."[3] Help me, Lord, thus to look up to thee, and thus to remember thee! Oh! that blessed scripture: "In all their affliction, he was afflicted; and the angel of his presence saved them; in his love, and in his pity, he redeemed them, and he bare them, and carried them all the days of old."[4] (Hawker, The Poor Man's Evening Portion, p. Jul 7)

Footnotes:
1. Hebrews 2:14.
2. Psalm 124.
3. Isaiah 53:3.
4. Isaiah 63:9.

61

Reading: Luke 17

"The apostles said to the Lord, "Increase our faith."" Luke 17:5

Did the apostles need so to pray? Then well may I. Oh! thou great Author and Finisher of our faith! I would look up to thee, with thankfulness, that thou hast granted even the smallest portion of faith to so unworthy a creature as I am. Surely, my soul, it is as great a miracle of grace that my God and Savior should have kindled belief in thy strong heart, amidst all the surrounding obstructions of sin and Satan which lay there; as when the miraculous fire from heaven, in answer to the prophet's prayer, came down and consumed the wetted sacrifice. I praise thee, my God and King, this day, in the recollection of this unspeakable, unmerited mercy. And though this faith in my heart still be but as a grain of mustard seed; though it be but as a spark in the ocean; though it be but as the drop of the dew, in comparison of the river; yet, blessed, precious Jesus! still this is faith, and it is thy gift. And is it not a token of thy favor? Is it not an earnest of the Holy Spirit, and a pledge of the promised inheritance? Babes in faith, as well as the strong in the Lord, are equally thine: for it is said, that as many as were ordained to eternal life believed;[1] and to as many as believed, thou gavest power to become the sons of God: so it is by thyself, blessed Redeemer! and not by the strength or weakness of the faith of thy people, their justification before God the Father is secured. Precious is that Scripture which tells us, that by thee all that believe, whether great faith or little faith – *all that believe*, are justified from all things.[2] But, my soul, while the consciousness of thy possessing the smallest evidences of faith in thy beloved, gives thee a joy unspeakable and full of glory, dost thou not blush to think what ungrateful returns thou art making to thy Redeemer in the littleness of thy faith in such a God and Savior? Whence is it that thine affections are so warm in a thousand lesser things, and so cold towards Jesus? Whence that his holy word thou so often hearest as though thou heardest not? Whence the ordinances of Jesus' house, the promises of his Scriptures, the visits of his grace; whence these pass again and again before thee, and thou remainest so cold and lifeless in thy affections? Whence that the temptations of Satan, the corruptions of thine heart, the allurements of the world, gain any influence upon thee? Whence that thou art so anxious about things that perish; about anything, about nothing deserving to be called interesting; whence so seldom at the court of the heavenly King, where thou oughtest to be found daily, hourly, waiting; and whence, under trials, or the want of answers at a mercy-seat, fretful, impatient, and misgiving – whence all these, and numberless other evils, but from the weakness and littleness of thy love *to* Jesus, thy trust *in* Jesus, thy dependence *upon* Jesus, and thy communion *with* Jesus? All, all arise out of this one sad cause, my soul, thine unbelief. Jesus! Master! look upon me, put the cry with earnestness in my heart, that I may unceasingly, with the Apostles' prayer, be sending forth this as the first and greatest petition of my whole soul – "Lord! increase my faith!" (Hawker, The Poor Man's Morning Portion, p. Apr 25)

Footnotes:
1. Acts 13:48.
2. Acts 13:32.

62

Reading: Mark 10

"... Immediately he could see and began to follow Jesus on the road." Mark 10:52

Blessed Bridegroom of thy Church!¹ how sweetly hast thou answered all the cavils of the *Pharisees*, and silenced all the fears of thy people, in teaching thy Church in the opening of this Chapter, that Jesus hath not put away his wife, notwithstanding all her shameful departures. Oh! for grace to cry out with the spouse, *my beloved is mine, and I am his!*²

Praises to the condescending grace of the Son of God, who receiveth now, as he received then, in the days of his flesh, little children. So, Lord must it be indeed thy grace to receive me, for I am but a child in understanding, and therefore I pray thee, thou tender Lord, to give me grace to sit at thy feet, and hear the blessed words which proceed out of thy mouth! And as thou hast taught me in the solemn example of this apparently promising youth, who for the love of this world's gain, could so readily give up Christ. Oh! for grace, to be kept from *the love of money, which is the root of all evil.*³ Bring my soul under the continual baptisms of the Holy Spirit;

and let my whole rejoicings be in the consciousness of an interest in that ransom, which my God and Savior hath given for many. Oh! thou glorious covenant of thy people! Thou hast indeed proved thyself to be Jehovah's Covenant in all thy words and works. Lord! I beseech thee give me grace to follow thee as *Bartimaeus* did; let me cast away, and cast off everything of mine; for all must be, as I am myself, unclean. Lord, be thou all my salvation and all my desire; give me spiritual sight, and enable me to follow thee in the way. (Hawker, Poor Man's New Testament Commentary: Matthew-John, p. 280)

Footnotes:
1. Isaiah 62:5; Revelation 21:9.
2. Song of Songs / Solomon 2:16.
3. 1 Timothy 6:10.

63

Reading: Matthew 19

"Good Master." Matthew 19:16

If the young man in the gospel used this title in speaking to our Lord, how much more fitly may I thus address him! He is indeed my Master in both senses, a ruling Master and a teaching Master. I delight to run upon his errands, and to sit at his feet. I am both his servant and his disciple, and count it my highest honor to own the double character. If he should ask me why I call him "good," I should have a ready answer. It is true that "there is none good but one, that is, God,"[1] but then he is God, and all the goodness of Deity shines forth in him. In my experience, I have found him good, so good, indeed, that all the good I have has come to me through him. He was good to me when I was dead in sin, for he raised me by his Spirit's power; he has been good to me in all my needs, trials, struggles, and sorrows. Never could there be a better Master, for his service is freedom, his rule is love: I wish I were one thousandth part as good a servant. When he teaches me as my Rabbi, he is unspeakably good, his doctrine is divine, his manner is condescending, his spirit is gentleness itself. No error mingles with his instruction – pure is the golden truth which he brings forth, and all his teachings lead to goodness, sanctifying as well as edifying the disciple. Angels find him a good Master and delight to pay their homage at his footstool. The ancient saints proved him to be a good Master, and each of them rejoiced to sing, "I am thy servant, O Lord!"[2] My own humble testimony must certainly be to the same effect. I will bear this witness before my friends and neighbors, for possibly they may be led by my testimony to seek my Lord Jesus as their Master. O that they would do so! They would never repent so wise a deed. If they would but take his easy yoke, they would find themselves in so royal a service that they would enlist in it for ever. (Spurgeon, p. Evening Jun 2)

Footnotes:
1. Mark 10:18.
2. Psalm 116:16.

64

Reading: Matthew 20

"The Son of Man will be handed over to the chief priests and scribes, and they will condemn him to death." Matthew 20:18

I pray the Reader not to overlook our Lord's delight in speaking of his approaching death. This is the third time the Lord reminds his disciples of it within a few Chapters. Chapter 16:21, and Chapter 17:22-23. And again in this place. Every act of Jesus testified his promptness to the work, as though he longed for it. *Lo! I come* (said Jesus) *to do thy will, O God. I delight to do it: yea, thy law is in the midst of my bowels.*[1] And when *Peter* out of love (though a mistaken love) for his master, wished it to be otherwise; Jesus rebuked him, yea, called him *Satan*, for what he said. Never did the meek and loving Savior ever drop such an expression before: so very intent was he on finishing the work his Father gave him to do, and so much displeased was he with anyone who wished it to be otherwise. Precious Lord Jesus! was this thine ardent love to thy spouse the Church, as one longing to bring her out of the prison-house of sin and Satan, though all the cataracts of divine wrath for sin were broken up, to be poured on thy sacred head! (Hawker, Poor Man's New Testament Commentary: Matthew-John, pp. 135–136)

Footnote:
1. Psalm 40:8.

65

Reading: Matthew 21

"And if you believe, you will receive whatever you ask for in prayer."
Matthew 21:22

Draw near, then, seeking soul, with boldness; not the boldness of a presumptuous, self-righteous man, but that of one chosen, called, pardoned, and justified. Draw near with the lowly boldness of a child – with the humble confidence of a son. Dear are you to your Father. Sweet is your voice to Him. Precious is your person, accepted in His Beloved. You cannot come too boldly; you cannot come too frequently – you cannot come with too large requests. You are coming to a King, that King your Father that Father viewing you in His beloved Son. Oh, hang not back. Stand not afar off. He now holds out the golden scepter, and says, "Come near; what is your request? Come with your temporal want. Come with your spiritual need. Ask what you will, it shall be granted you. I have an open hand, and a large heart." Is it your desire – "Lord, I want more grace to glorify You. I want more simplicity of mind, and singleness of eye. I want a more holy, upright, honest walk. I want more meekness, patience, lowliness, submission. I want to know more of Jesus, to see more of His glory, to feel more of His preciousness, and to live more simply upon His fullness. I want more of the sanctifying, sealing, witnessing, and anointing influences of the Spirit"? Blessed, holy desires! It is the Spirit making intercession in you according to the will of God; and entering into the holiest by the blood of Jesus, the Lord will fulfill the desires of your heart, even to the half of kingdom.

Watch diligently against the least declension in the spirit of prayer. If there be declension here, there will also be declension in every part and department of the work of the Spirit in your soul. It is prayer that keeps every grace of the Spirit in active, holy, and healthy exercise. It is the stream, so to speak, that supplies refreshing vigor and nourishment to all the plants of grace. It is true, that the fountain-head of all spiritual life and "grace to help in time of need,"[1] is Christ; "for it pleased the Father that in Him should all fullness dwell."[2] And Paul's encouragement to the Philippians was, "My God shall supply all your need, according to His riches in glory by Christ Jesus."[3] But the channel through which all grace comes is prayer – ardent, wrestling, importunate, believing prayer. Suffer this channel to be dry – permit any object to narrow or close it up – and the effect will be a withering and decay of the life of God in the soul.

Guard, then, against the slightest decline of prayer in the soul. If prayer – family prayer, social prayer, most of all, closet prayer, is declining with you, no further evidence is needed of your being in a backsliding state of mind. There may not yet have been the outward departure, but you are in the way to it – and nothing but a return to prayer will save you. Oh, what alarm, what fearfulness and trembling, should this thought occasion in a child of God, "I am on my way to an awful departure from God! Such is the state of my soul at this moment, such my present state of mind, such the loss of my spirituality, such the hold which the world has upon my affections, there is no length in sin to which I may not now go, there is no iniquity which I may not now commit. The breakers are full in view, and my poor weak vessel is heading to and rapidly nearing them." What can shield you from the commission of that sin? What can keep you from wounding Jesus afresh? What can preserve you from foundering and making shipwreck of your faith? But an immediate and fervent return to prayer. Prayer is your only safety. Prayer is for grace to help in your time of need. Prayer is for reviving grace, for quickening, restraining and sanctifying grace. Prayer is to keep us from falling, to hold us up in the slippery paths. Prayer is for the lowly mind, for the contrite spirit, for the broken heart, for the soft, and close, and humble walk with God. (Winslow, Evening Thoughts, p. Nov 2)

Footnotes:
1. Hebrews 4:16.
2. Colossians 1:19.
3. Philippians 4:19.

66

Reading: Luke 18-19

"Zacchaeus, hurry and come down because today it is necessary for me to stay at your house." Luke 19:5

Precious Jesus! what an instance is here of the freeness, fulness, and sovereignty of thy grace! And was there *a needs be*, O Lord, that thou shouldst go to the place where this publican was? *a needs be* to look up and see him? *a needs be* to call him? and *a needs be* to abide at his house? Is this thy manner, O Lord, in calling sinners? So then it was not Zacchaeus seeking Jesus, but Jesus seeking Zacchaeus. His curiosity, as he thought, led him thither; but it was the prevenient grace of Jesus in the poor man's heart that first awakened that curiosity in him. And did Jesus seek Zacchaeus, call Zacchaeus, incline Zacchaeus to receive him, and bring salvation to his heart and house that blessed day? Oh! then for grace to see, and enjoy Jesus in all. Yea, I see, Lord, now plain enough, that all is thine; and of thine own, all we give is from thee. When first my heart felt inclined to seek Jesus, it was Jesus who inclined my heart to this Christ seeking. Never should I have looked on thee, nor felt an inclination to see thee, hadst thou not first looked on me, and given me that desire.

And what it was first, so is it now, in all the after enjoyments of thy sight and of thy presence. If I am at any time looking after thee, I may cry out with Abraham's hand-maid, "Thou, Lord, seest me,"[1] and art looking after me. For never, even after all my knowledge of thee, should I look to thee, with an eye of desire, except the eye of Jesus glance on me as it did on Peter, in quickening and awakening grace. Oh! then, thou dear Lord! let me daily, hourly hear thy voice calling me down from all creature-concerns, and creature-confidences, to receive my Lord; and be thou constrained by thy love to come, not as the wayfaring man, to tarry but for the night, but to abide, and dwell, and never more depart from me. Be thou my God, and make me thy servant forever. (Hawker, The Poor Man's Evening Portion, p. Nov 20)

Footnote:
1. Genesis 16:13.

67

Reading: Mark 11

"Have faith in God." Mark 11:22

Faith is the foot of the soul by which it can march along the road of the commandments. Love can make the feet move more swiftly; but faith is the foot which carries the soul. Faith is the oil enabling the wheels of holy devotion and of earnest piety to move well; and without faith the wheels are taken from the chariot, and we drag heavily. With faith I can do all things; without faith I shall neither have the inclination nor the power to do anything in the service of God. If you would find the men who serve God the best, you must look for the men of the most faith. Little faith will save a man, but little faith cannot do great things for God. Poor Little-faith could not have fought "Apollyon;" it needed "Christian" to do that. Poor Little-faith could not have slain "Giant Despair;" it required "Great-heart's" arm to knock that monster down. Little faith will go to heaven most certainly, but it often has to hide itself in a nut-shell, and it frequently loses all but its jewels. Little-faith says, "It is a rough road, beset with sharp thorns, and full of dangers; I am afraid to go;" but Great-faith remembers the promise, "Thy shoes shall be iron and brass; as thy days, so shall thy strength be:"[1] and so she boldly ventures. Little-faith stands desponding, mingling her tears with the flood; but Great-faith sings, "When thou passest through the waters, I will be with thee; and through the rivers, they shall not overflow thee:"[2] and she fords the stream at once. Would you be comfortable and happy? Would you enjoy religion? Would you have the religion of cheerfulness and not that of gloom? Then "have faith in God." If you love darkness, and are satisfied to dwell in gloom and misery, then be content with little faith; but if you love the sunshine, and would sing songs of rejoicing, covet earnestly this best gift, "great faith." (Spurgeon, p. Morning Mar 7)

Footnotes:
1. Deuteronomy 33:25.
2. Isaiah 43:2.

68

Reading: John 12

"Isaiah said these things because he saw his glory and spoke about him." John 12:41

It will be observed, that John affirms of Isaiah that he saw the glory of Christ. The glory of the Redeemer has ever been an object visible to the spiritual eye. What the evangelist here records of the prophet, he also avows of himself and his fellow-disciples. "And the Word was made flesh, and dwelt among us, and we beheld His glory."[1] Here is a point of vital moment, entering deeply into the very soul of experimental [experiential] Christianity. May the Spirit of all truth give us a clear and solemn perception of it![2] If a man sees not the glory of Christ, we hesitate not to say of him, that with regard to all other spiritual objects he is totally blind – he is yet a stranger to the illuminating grace of the Holy Spirit. To see the Redeemer's glory, the eye must be spiritual; a spiritual object being only discerned by a spiritual organ. Hence the apostle prays in behalf of the Ephesian Christians, "That the God of our Lord Jesus Christ, the Father of glory, may give unto you the Spirit of wisdom and revelation in the knowledge of Him: that the eyes of your understanding being enlightened."³ And enlightened by the Spirit of God, the believer beholds the glory of Jesus. Brought to see no glory in himself, yes, nothing but deformity in that on which the eye once so complacently rested, the glory of the Redeemer, as it is reflected in His person, in His atoning blood and justifying righteousness, His infinite fullness of grace to pardon and to sanctify, fills now the entire scope of his moral vision, and lifts his soul in admiring and adoring thoughts of the holiness and love of God!

More than this, such is its transforming influence, he comes to be a partaker, in a degree, of that very glory which has arrested his eye and ravished his heart. On him the glory of the Lord has shone, the Sun of Righteousness has risen – he rises from the dust, and shines arrayed in garments of light from Christ's reflecting light. A sight of Jesus assimilates the soul to His Spirit; a contemplation of His beauty transforms the believer more and more into "the child of the light;" and thus perpetually "looking unto Jesus,"⁴ the path he treads kindles and glows with an increasing effulgence, until its luster expands into perfect cloudless day. "We all, with open face beholding as in a glass the glory of the Lord, are changed into the same image, from glory to glory, even as by the Spirit of the Lord."⁵ The medium through which the spiritual eye beholds the glory of Christ is faith. It is a hidden glory until the Eternal Spirit imparts this mighty principle to the soul. The eye of reason cannot discern it – the eye of intellect and of sense cannot behold it – it remains a veiled thing, "dark with excessive brightness," until God the Holy Spirit utters His voice, "Let there be light."⁶ "Abraham," says Christ, "rejoiced to see my day; and he saw it, and was glad."⁷ At that remote period, how did he see it? – by faith. Through the long and dreary vista of advancing ages he saw the day dawning, the sun rising. By faith he beheld Jesus approaching. He saw His blood, His righteousness, and His own interest there, "and he was glad." Oh yes, a sight of Jesus by faith – be it distant and dim, be it shadowy and imperfect – fills the soul with ineffable gladness, lights up its onward way, sweetens its solitude, enlivens its loneliness, and soothes it amid its deepest sorrows.

Isaiah not only beheld the glory of Christ, but he also "spoke of it." He could not but speak of that which he saw and felt. And who can behold the glory of the Redeemer, and not speak of it? Who can see His beauty, and not extol it – who can taste His love, and not laud it? "Come," will be the invitation, "see a man who told me all things that ever I did: is not this the Christ?"[8] The church of old, as her eye wandered over the beauties of her Lord, broke forth in expressions of wonder and praise; and, after particularizing and extolling these beauties, she then exclaims, as if all language were exhausted, "Yes, He is altogether lovely. This is my beloved, and this is my friend."[9] "In His temple does every one speak of His glory." Yes, the saints of the Most High must speak of the King in His beauty. They are constrained to show forth His praise, and tell of His love and loveliness, who is to them more precious than the gold of Ophir; yes, dearer than life itself. The Pharisee may murmur, the worldling may scorn, and the coldhearted professor may rebuke; yet, "if these should hold their peace," who have been redeemed by His most precious blood, and who are looking forward to His second appearing, as an event which shall conform them to His likeness, "the stones would immediately cry out."[10] (Winslow, Evening Thoughts, p. Sep 5)

Footnotes:
1. John 1:14.
2. John 16:13.
3. Ephesians 1:17-18.
4. Hebrews 12:2.
5. 2 Corinthians 3:18.
6. Genesis 1:3.

7. John 8:56.
8. John 4:29.
9. Song of Songs / Solomon 5:16.
10. Luke 19:40.

69

Reading: Mark 12

Pause my soul over the many precious contents in this blessed Chapter! Both the Jewish nation, and the Jewish church, have been as the Lord's vineyard. Oh! the boundless grace of Jehovah in setting apart that people with whom he deposited his Ordinances; *whose are the fathers, and of whom as concerning the flesh* Christ *came, who is over all* God *blessed forever, Amen.*[1] But oh! the wonderful provocations of Israel, in slighting the Lord's servants rising early and speaking, but regarding them not; till at length they killed the Lord of life and glory! But, Reader! are we then by nature or by practice better than they? Oh! no, in no wise. The Lord hath concluded all under sin, that the righteousness of God, which is by faith of Jesus Christ, might be given to them that believe.[2] *Oh! the depth of the riches, both of the wisdom and knowledge of* God![3]

My soul! behold thy Lord attacked in every way, by men calling him *Rabbi;* and professing great regard to his person, for his teaching the way of God in truth; and by *Pharisee* and *Sadducee,* by *Herodians* and by *Scribes,* aiming to catch him in his words! Oh! thou divine and Almighty Teacher, cause thy blessed truths in this chapter to sink deep into my heart! Lord! be thou everlastingly blessed for thy gracious discoveries concerning the glorious truths of thy resurrection. Lord! be thou my resurrection, and my life! Give me to know Israel's God in covenant as one Lord! And oh! give me grace to love Him in his threefold character of Person, Father, Son, and Holy Spirit, *with all my heart, with all my soul, with all my mind, and with all my strength*.[4] And in the love of God may my affections find sweet directions, to the love of my neighbor. So will David's Lord be my Lord, and his Christ my Christ. And like the poor widow, the Lord's treasury will have my whole living; since all I have, and all I am, are the Lord's, and of His own only do I give him. (Hawker, Poor Man's New Testament Commentary: Matthew-John, pp. 293–294)

Footnotes:
1. Romans 9:5.
2. Romans 3:22.
3. Romans 11:33.
4. Luke 10:27; Deuteronomy 6:5; Matthew 22:37.

70

Reading: Matthew 22

"*What think ye of Christ?*" Matthew 22:42 (AKJV)

The great test of your soul's health is, *What think you of Christ?* Is he to you "fairer than the children of men" – "the chief among ten thousand" – the "altogether lovely"?[1] Wherever Christ is thus esteemed, all the faculties of the spiritual man exercise themselves with energy. I will judge of your piety by this barometer: does Christ stand high or low with you? If you have thought little of Christ, if you have been content to live without his presence, if you have cared little for his honor, if you have been neglectful of his laws, then I know that your soul is sick – God grant that it may not be sick unto death! But if the first thought of your spirit has been, how can I honor Jesus? If the daily desire of your soul has been, "O that I knew where I might find him!" I tell you that you may have a thousand infirmities, and even scarcely know whether you are a child of God at all, and yet I am persuaded, beyond a doubt, that you are safe, since Jesus is great in your esteem. I care not for thy rags, what thinkest thou of *his* royal apparel? I care not for thy wounds, though they bleed in torrents, what thinkest thou of his wounds?

are they like glittering rubies in thine esteem? I think none the less of thee, though thou liest like Lazarus on the dunghill, and the dogs do lick thee – I judge thee not by thy poverty: what thinkest thou of the King in his beauty? Has he a glorious high throne in thy heart? Wouldest thou set him higher if thou couldest? Wouldest thou be willing to die if thou couldest but add another trumpet to the strain which proclaims his praise? Ah! then it is well with thee. Whatever thou mayest think of thyself, if Christ be great to thee, thou shalt be with him ere long.

> *"Though all the world my choice deride,*
> *Yet Jesus shall my portion be;*
> *For I am pleased with none beside,*
> *The fairest of the fair is he"*
> (Spurgeon, p. Evening Dec 29)

Footnote:
1. Psalm 45:2; Song of Songs / Solomon 5:10.

71

Reading: Luke 20

"How can they say that the Christ is the son of David?" Luke 20:41

Our Lord, having now for ever driven from the field of disputation, the whole body of Scribes, Pharisees, and Sadducees, takes occasion to lead to a subject highly interesting, that he might not only instruct his Church in that great doctrine of his double nature, God and Man, in One Person; but at the same time, pass his farewell sentence of condemnation upon the Scribes of that day, and the Pharisees, and self-righteous of every day, in all future generations; Jesus therefore puts forth a question respecting the relationship between *David* king of Israel and the Messiah, which was foretold as *David's Son* after the flesh. He takes for granted, that none among them had any question, as to the coming of Christ; but he questions, if they knew in what sense it was that he was *David's* Son. They were struck dumb at the question; and from not being taught of God, were unable to answer it. But, Reader! how truly blessed is our privilege, when taught of God. You and I perfectly know, and are assured, from that infallible teacher, that Christ is both the *root* and the *offspring* of *David*.[1] For as God, *One with the* Father *over all* God *blessed forever;*[2] he is, and must be God: David's *root*, and the *maker of all things*. And as man he is the *offspring*, which as a *branch*, was promised to grow out of his roots:[3] Precious Jesus! hadst thou not been *both*, what would have become of me? Lord I hail thee, as the Lord my righteousness! Reader! do not hastily turn away from the solemn sentence Christ pronounceth on the Scribes of old. Awful as the case of all sinners must be, who live and die in their sins; yet of all the tremendous judgments pronounced on the Christless, you see, by Christ's own words, the greater damnation will be on those who from self-righteousness, lessen in their esteem the infinitely precious value of Christ's blood and salvation; as if the necessity of Christ's sufferings were not so highly needed to recommend them to God![4] (Hawker, Poor Man's New Testament Commentary: Matthew-John, pp. 487–488)

Footnotes:
1. Revelation 22:16.
2. Romans 9:5.
3. Isaiah 11:1.
4. Isaiah 65:5.

72

Reading: Luke 21

"Watch ye therefore, and pray always, that ye may be accounted worthy to escape all these things that shall come to pass, and to stand before the Son of Man." Luke 21:36

How closely and beautifully has our dear Lord connected together these two important Christian duties – "Watch and pray!" The one as necessary as the other is sublime. Watchfulness implying uncertainty as to time; prayer expressive of an earnest desire to be found in an appropriate attitude for the event. "Therefore, be you ready also; for in such an hour as you do not think, the Son of Man comes."[1] "Behold, I come as a thief. Blessed is he that watches, and keeps his garments." Surely if our affections were supremely fixed on Jesus – were He to us as the "chief among ten thousand,"[2] and did we really feel in our hearts the sentiment which our lips so often utter, "Whom have I in heaven but You? And there is none upon earth that I desire beside You,"[3] the return of our Lord would be to us a matter of most delightsome expectation and wearisome desire. Our earnest prayer would oftener be, "Why are

Your chariot-wheels so long in coming? Come, Lord Jesus, come quickly!"

Dear reader, are you prepared for the coming of the Lord? Are you ready to enter in with Him to the marriage supper? Are you a professor? Have you grace renewing, humbling, sanctifying, Christ-exalting grace in your heart? Is your preparation one of principle, one of habit? Will it abide the searching scrutiny of that day? Examine and see. Take nothing for granted, in deciding a matter so solemn, and involving interests so momentous. Christ must be all in all to you – the entire ground-work and fabric of your salvation. Mere notions of truth – external membership with the church – sacraments – regular attendance upon means – punctilious observance of days, and forms, and ceremonies, in themselves are no fit preparation for this awful event. As the fruit of a living faith in Jesus, they are valuable; but standing alone, without repentance towards God and faith in the Lord Jesus Christ, they are the wood, the hay, the stubble which the last fire will consume.

Believer in Jesus! The day of your redemption draws near! The Lord is at hand. Behold, the Judge stands at the door. The days we live in are eventful – the times are perilous. The signs, thickening and darkening around us, are deeply and fearfully significant. We are standing on the eve of events perhaps more awful than the world has ever seen. A period of glory for the church, brighter than has yet shone upon her, and a period of woe to the world, darker than has yet cast its shadows upon it, seems rapidly approaching. Then, "let us not sleep as do others, but let us watch and be sober."[4] "And that, knowing the time, that now it is high time to awake out of sleep; for now is our salvation nearer than when we believed. The night is far spent, the day is at hand."[5] "Watch you, therefore: for you know not when the Master of the house comes; at even, or at midnight, or at the cock-crowing, or in the morning: lest coming suddenly, He find you sleeping."[6] Oh, to blend the steady thought of our Redeemer's coming with every present duty, privilege, and effort, how would it hallow, cheer, and dignify us, consecrating by one of the most solemn motives the lowliest work of faith and the feeblest labor of love!

Thus, too, would there be a growing preparedness of mind for the judgments which are yet to come upon the earth. "For there shall be great tribulation, such as was not since the beginning of the world to this time, no, nor ever shall be." "Men's hearts failing them for fear, and for looking after those things which are coming on the earth; for the powers of heaven shall be shaken. And then shall they see the Son of man coming in a cloud, with power and great glory. And when these things begin to come to pass, then look up, and lift up your heads; for your redemption draws near." (Winslow, Evening Thoughts, p. Aug 16)

Footnotes:
1. Matthew 24:43-51.
2. Song of Songs / Solomon 5:10.
3. Psalm 73:25.
4. 1 Thessalonians 5:6.
5. Romans 13:11-12.
6. Mark 13:35.

73

Reading: Matthew 23

"In the same way, on the outside you seem righteous to people, but inside you are full of hypocrisy and lawlessness." Matthew 23:28

One word more, and I will relieve the Reader's attention. How did this generation of vipers manifest their serpentine hatred to Christ, and bring upon themselves those awful denunciations? Not for their immoralities, for they prided themselves in being highly moral. Not for their neglect of their public or private worship. For they did both. Neither were they chargeable, as far as outward actions went, with the common vices of drunkenness, adultery, and the like. What was it then, which brought down upon them the Lord's severest judgments? Certainly, nothing more or less, than by this Pharisaical righteousness, teaching the people to slight the person and work of Jesus, as what were unnecessary for acceptance with God. They compassed sea and land the Lord told them, to make one proselyte, and when this was done, they made him two-fold more the child of hell, than themselves. That is, they labored to undermine the necessity of salvation by Christ, in setting up, and teaching others to do the same, a righteousness of their own: and thus by denying the fall of man, and the necessity of a recovery by grace, they set up the kingdom of Satan, and like children of hell, fought against the kingdom of grace.

Reader! pause over the awful subject! If such be the views which arise out of Pharisaical righteousness; we can no longer wonder at any of our Lord's expressions in this Chapter. And under the conviction, that nothing can be more in opposition to the very first principles of the Gospel; nothing more fatal to the humblings of grace; nothing which equally tends to make the cross of Christ of little worth, and the righteousness of Christ of no effect; I would say for myself, and every one, whose present and everlasting welfare I feel concerned, —From all self-righteousness, spiritual pride, hardness of heart, and contempt of thy word and commandments, Good Lord! deliver us! (Hawker, Poor Man's New Testament Commentary: Matthew-John, pp. 157–158)

74

Reading: Mark 13

"Jesus said to him, "Do you see these great buildings? Not one stone will be left upon another – all will be thrown down." Mark 13:2

When we read, as in this scripture, of Jesus departing from the temple, and connect with it that it was his farewell departure, for he never again entered it, what solemn thoughts it awakens? When the Lord departs, woe to that land, woe to that house or family, where the Lord's gracious presence is not. No sooner had *Lot* departed from *Sodom* than the next account is the destruction of it.[1] And who shall say how much the Christless owe in being saved from instant ruin, both in nations, and cities, and families, from; the seed of Christ living in the midst of them.

This *second* temple, though so vastly inferior to the glory of the *first*, or *Solomon's* temple, so called, that the antient men who had seen the former, wept at beholding this latter.[2] And see the Lord's promise in consequence thereof[3] and which was literally fulfilled when the Son of God in our nature entered it: this second temple was a wonderful building. It had been repaired by *Herod;* and

Josephus, the Jewish historian, saith, that some of the stones were of a magnitude even to *forty-five cubits* long, *five* high, and *six* broad. Jesus declared that such should be the desolation of the place, when the Lord visited it for the rejection of Christ, that not one of these immense stones should be left upon another. And we are told in history, that when *Titus*, under whose army *Jerusalem* was sacked, heard of this prophecy of Christ, he endeavored to counteract it; but such was the impetuosity of his army, that no orders could restrain them, and Christ's prediction was literally fulfilled. (Hawker, Poor Man's New Testament Commentary: Matthew-John, pp. 294–295)

Footnotes:
1. Genesis 19:22–24.
2. Ezra 3:12-13.
3. Haggai 2:1–9.

75

Reading: Matthew 24

"They didn't know until the flood came and swept them all away. This is the way the coming of the Son of Man will be." Matthew 24:39

Universal was the doom, neither rich nor poor escaped: the learned and the illiterate, the admired and the abhorred, the religious and the profane, the old and the young, all sank in one common ruin. Some had doubtless ridiculed the patriarch – where now their merry jests? Others had threatened him for his zeal which they counted madness – where now their boastings and hard speeches? The critic who judged the old man's work is drowned in the same sea which covers his sneering companions. Those who spoke patronizingly of the good man's fidelity to his convictions, but shared not in them, have sunk to rise no more, and the workers who for pay helped to build the wondrous ark, are all lost also. The flood swept them all away, and made no single exception.[1] Even so, out of Christ, final destruction is sure to every man of woman born; no rank, possession, or character, shall suffice to save a single soul who has not believed in the Lord Jesus.[2] My soul, behold this wide-spread judgment and tremble at it.

How marvelous the general apathy! they were all eating and drinking, marrying and giving in marriage, till the awful morning dawned. There was not one wise man upon earth out of the ark. Folly duped the whole race, folly as to self-preservation – the most foolish of all follies. Folly in doubting the most true God – the most malignant of fooleries. Strange, my soul, is it not? All men are negligent of their souls till grace gives them reason, then they leave their madness and act like rational beings, but not till then.

All, blessed be God, were safe in the ark, no ruin entered there. From the huge elephant down to the tiny mouse all were safe. The timid hare was equally secure with the courageous lion, the helpless cony as safe as the laborious ox. All are safe in Jesus. My soul, art thou in him? (Spurgeon, p. Evening Nov 1)

Footnote:
1. Genesis, chapters 6-7.
2. John 3:18.

76

Reading: Matthew 25

"And at midnight there was a cry made, Behold, the bridegroom cometh, go ye out to meet him." Matthew 25:6 (AKJV)

When Jesus, the bridegroom of his Church, first came, it was in a moment sudden and unexpected, like the surprise at a midnight hour. And when Jesus cometh to any of his people, it is unlooked for. Indeed, it is always midnight in the soul of a sinner, when the cry is made! But how blessed is the cry, when a poor, lost, perishing sinner is advanced to the midnight of death, on the verge of an approaching eternity, and in that season hears the voice of the Son of God and lives! How many, like the thief on the cross, or like the jailer at *Philippi*,[1] have been surprised into grace at such seasons, by the sovereignty of him, "who calleth things that are not as though they were!"[2] Precious Jesus! in all the circumstances of life, in the midnight of nature, the midnight of carnal security, the midnight of sleep, in which even thy dear children are so liable to be found, oh! that we may hear thy voice, and go forth to meet thee! And, Lord! let the going forth of thy redeemed be, not with the lamp of a profession, but with the enlightened oil of grace, that we may meet thee with all our affections alive, to hail and welcome thy coming; so that "at midnight, or cock-crowing, or in the morning," when Jesus saith, "Behold I come quickly," our souls may cry out, in joyful reply, "Even so; come, Lord Jesus!"[3] (Hawker, The Poor Man's Evening Portion, p. Dec 13)

Footnotes:
1. Acts 16:25-34.
2. Romans 4:17.
3. Revelation 22:20.

77

Reading: Mark 14

"And when he thought thereon, he wept." Mark 14:72 (AKJV)

It has been thought by some that as long as Peter lived, the fountain of his tears began to flow whenever he remembered his denying his Lord. It is not unlikely that it was so, for his sin was very great, and grace in him had afterwards a perfect work. This same experience is common to all the redeemed family according to the degree in which the Spirit of God has removed the natural heart of stone. We, like Peter, remember *our boastful promise*: "Though all men shall forsake thee, yet will not I."[1] We eat our own words with the bitter herbs of repentance. When we think of what we vowed we would be, and of what we have been, we may weep whole showers of grief. He thought on *his denying his Lord*. The place in which he did it, the little cause which led him into such heinous sin, the oaths and blasphemies with which he sought to confirm his falsehood, and the dreadful hardness of heart which drove him to do so again and yet again. Can we, when we are reminded of our sins, and their exceeding sinfulness, remain stolid and stubborn? Will we not make our house a Bochim, and cry unto the Lord for renewed assurances of pardoning love? May we never take a dry-eyed look at sin, lest ere long we have a tongue parched in the flames of hell. Peter also thought upon *his Master's look of love*. The Lord followed up the cock's warning voice with an admonitory look of sorrow, pity, and love. That glance was never out of Peter's mind so long as he lived. It was far more effectual than ten thousand sermons would have been without the Spirit. The penitent apostle would be sure to weep when he recollected the *Savior's full forgiveness*, which restored him to his former place.[2] To think that we have offended so kind and good a Lord is more than sufficient reason for being constant weepers. Lord, smite our rocky hearts, and make the waters flow. (Spurgeon, p. Morning Jul 30)

Footnotes:
1. Matthew 26:35.
2. John 21.

78

Reading: Matthew 26

"Going a little farther, he fell facedown and prayed ..." Matthew 26:39

There are several instructive features in our Savior's prayer in his hour of trial. It was *lonely prayer*. He withdrew even from his three favored disciples. Believer, be much in solitary prayer, especially in times of trial. Family prayer, social prayer, prayer in the Church, will not suffice, these are very precious, but the best beaten spice will smoke in your censer in your private devotions, where no ear hears but God's.

It was *humble prayer*. Luke says he knelt, but another evangelist says he "fell on his face." Where, then, must be THY place, thou humble servant of the great Master? What dust and ashes should cover thy head! Humility gives us good foot-hold in prayer. There is no hope of prevalence with God unless we abase ourselves that he may exalt us in due time.[1]

It was *filial prayer*. "Abba, Father." You will find it a stronghold in the day of trial to plead your adoption. You have no rights as a subject, you have forfeited them by your treason; but nothing can forfeit a child's right to a father's protection. Be not afraid to say, "My Father, hear my cry."

Observe that it was *persevering prayer*. He prayed three times. Cease not until you prevail. Be as the importunate widow, whose continual coming earned what her first supplication could not win.[2] Continue in prayer, and watch in the same with thanksgiving.

Lastly, *it was the prayer of resignation*. "Nevertheless, not as I will, but as thou wilt." Yield, and God yields. Let it be as God wills, and God will determine for the best. Be thou content to leave thy prayer in his hands, who knows when to give, and how to give, and what to give, and what to withhold. So, pleading, earnestly, importunately, yet with humility and resignation, thou shalt surely prevail.[3] (Spurgeon, p. Morning Mar 22)

Footnotes:
1. 1 Peter 5:6.
2. Luke 18:1-8.
3. See also James 5:16.

79

Reading: John 13

"*He began to wash the disciples' feet.*" John 13:5

The Lord Jesus loves his people so much, that every day he is still doing for them much that is analogous to washing their soiled feet. Their poorest actions he accepts; their deepest sorrow he feels; their slenderest wish he hears, and their every transgression he forgives. He is still their servant as well as their Friend and Master. He not only performs majestic deeds for them, as wearing the miter on his brow, and the precious jewels glittering on his breastplate, and standing up to plead for them, but humbly, patiently, he yet goes about among his people with the basin and the towel. He does this when he puts away from us day by day our constant infirmities and sins. Last night, when you bowed the knee, you mournfully confessed that much of your conduct was not worthy of your profession; and even tonight, you must mourn afresh that you have fallen again into the selfsame folly and sin from which special grace delivered you long ago; and yet Jesus will have great patience with you; he will hear your confession of sin; he will say, "I will, be thou clean";[1] he will again apply the blood of sprinkling, and speak peace to your conscience, and remove every spot. It is a great act of eternal love when Christ once for all absolves the sinner, and puts him into the family of God; but what condescending patience there is when the Savior with much long-suffering bears the oft recurring follies of his wayward disciple; day by day, and hour by hour, washing away the multiplied transgressions of his erring but yet beloved child! To dry up a flood of rebellion is something marvelous, but to endure the constant dropping of repeated offences – to bear with a perpetual trying of patience, this is divine indeed! While we find comfort and peace in our Lord's daily cleansing, its legitimate influence upon us will be to increase our watchfulness, and quicken our desire for holiness. *Is it so?* (Spurgeon, p. Evening Oct 24)

Footnote:
1. Luke 5:13; Matthew 8:3.

80

Reading: Luke 22

"... his sweat became like drops of blood falling to the ground."
Luke 22:44

The mental pressure arising from our Lord's struggle with temptation, so forced his frame to an unnatural excitement, that his pores sent forth great drops of blood which fell down to the ground. This proves *how tremendous must have been the weight of sin* when it was able to crush the Savior so that he distilled great drops of blood! This demonstrates *the mighty power of his love.* It is a very pretty observation of old Isaac Ambrose that the gum which exudes from the tree without cutting is always the best. This precious camphire-tree yielded most sweet spices when it was wounded under the knotty whips, and when it was pierced by the nails on the cross; but see, it giveth forth its best spice when there is no whip, no nail, no wound. This sets forth the *voluntariness of Christ's sufferings,* since without a lance the blood flowed freely. No need to put on the leech, or apply the knife; it flows spontaneously. No need for the rulers to cry, "Spring up, O well;" of itself it flows in crimson torrents. If men suffer great pain of mind apparently the blood rushes to the heart. The cheeks are pale; a fainting fit comes on; the blood has gone inward as if to nourish the inner man while passing through its trial. But see our Savior in his agony; he is so utterly oblivious of self, that instead of his agony driving his blood to the heart to nourish himself, it drives it outward to bedew the earth. The agony of Christ, inasmuch as it pours him out upon the ground, pictures the fulness of the offering which he made for men.

Do we not perceive how intense must have been the wrestling through which he passed, and will we not hear its voice to us? *"Ye have not yet resisted unto blood, striving against sin."*[1] Behold the great Apostle and High Priest of our profession, and sweat even to blood rather than yield to the great tempter of your souls. (Spurgeon, p. Morning Mar 23)

Footnote:
1. Hebrews 12:4.

81

Reading: John 14

"Jesus told him, "I am the way, the truth, and the life. No one comes to the Father except through me." John 14:6

Not the least costly blessing, flowing from the vital power of the atoning blood, is the life and potency which it imparts to true prayer. The believer's path to communion with God is called the "new and living way" because it is the way of the life-blood of the risen and living Savior. There could be no spiritual life in prayer but for the vitality in the atoning blood, which secures its acceptance. Not even could the Holy Spirit inspire the soul with one breath of true prayer, were not the atonement of the Son of God provided. Oh, how faintly do we know the wonders that are in, and the blessings that spring from, the life-procuring blood of our incarnate God! Touching the article of prayer – I approach to God, oppressed with sins, my heart crushed with sorrow, my spirit trembling; shame and confusion covering my face, my mouth dumb before Him. At that moment the blood of Jesus is presented, faith beholds it, faith receives it, faith pleads it! There is life and power in that blood, and lo! in an instant my trembling soul is enabled to take hold of God's strength and be at peace with Him, and it is at peace. Of all the Christian privileges upon earth, none can surpass, none can compare with, the privilege of fellowship with God. And yet how restricted is this privilege in the experience of multitudes! And why? simply in consequence of their vague, imperfect, and contracted views of the connection of true prayer with the living blood of Jesus. And yet, oh, what nearness to, what communion with, the Father, may the meanest, the feeblest, the most unworthy child at all times and in all circumstances have, who simply and believingly makes use of the blood of Christ! You approach without an argument or a plea. You have many sins to confess, sorrows to unveil, many requests to urge, many blessings to crave; and yet the deep consciousness of your utter vileness, the remembrance of mercies abused, of base, ungrateful requitals made, seals your lips, and you are dumb before God. Your overwhelmed spirit exclaims, "Oh that I knew where I might find him! that I might come even to his seat! I would order my cause before him, and fill my mouth with arguments."[1] And now the Holy Spirit brings atoning blood to your help. You see this to be the one argument, the only plea that can prevail with God. You use it – you urge it – you wrestle with it. God admits it, is moved by it, and you are blest! Let, then the life-power of the blood encourage you to cultivate more diligently habitual communion with God.[2] With sinking spirits, with even discouragement and difficulty, you may approach His Divine Majesty, and converse with Him as with a Father, resting your believing eye where He rests His complacent eye – upon the blood of Jesus. Oh the blessedness, the power, the magic influence of prayer! Believer! you grasp the key that opens every chamber of God's heart, when your tremulous faith takes hold of the blood of the covenant, and pleads it in prayer with God. It is impossible that God can then refuse you. The voice of the living blood pleads louder for you than all other voices can plead against you. Give yourself, then, unto prayer – this sacred charm of sorrow, this divine talisman of hope. (Winslow, Morning Thoughts, p. Dec 10)

Footnotes:
1. Job 23:3-4.
2. 1 John 2:2; Hebrews 4:14-16.

82

Reading: John 15

Reader! do not fail to observe the intimate oneness and union between Christ and his Church. The vine and its branches are not more closely formed in one, than Jesus and his people. Indeed, there are no figures, no images, either in nature or art, which can fully come up to the resemblance. All figures must fall short of the reality. But while we observe the closeness of union, let you and I be still more anxious to know whether we are the happy partakers of it. Are we indeed One with Christ, and Christ with us? *He that is joined to the* Lord *is one* Spirit.[1] One principle actuates both. What Jesus loves, we love; what Jesus hates, we hate. We look to Jesus for all things, and desire to eye Jesus in all things. Moreover, if one Spirit be in both, we shall undertake nothing but in his strength, and seek nothing but his glory. And as the branch wholly hangs upon, and is kept alive by the vine, so all our graces are kept alive by life *in* Jesus, and communications *from* Jesus. Oh! for grace to know these things in a lively, active, spiritual enjoyment of them, that we may be increasing in desires after him, and loosening from everything that is not in him, till we come to see him as he is, and dwell with him forever.

Blessed Holy Comforter of the Lord's people![2] Gracious Spirit of truth to lead into all truth![3] Oh! grant to me the knowledge of my Lord under all his sweet and precious offices! Send out Lord! thy light and thy truth to guide my poor soul continually! And, oh! for the daily, hourly renewing of the Holy Spirit, to be shed abundantly upon the churches and people, through Jesus Christ our Savior. Amen. (Hawker, Poor Man's New Testament Commentary: Matthew-John, p. 667)

Footnotes:
1. 1 Corinthians 6:17.
2. John 14:16.
3. John 16:13.

83

Reading: John 16

"He shall take of mine, and shall show it unto you." John 16:15 (AKJV)

There are times when all the promises and doctrines of the Bible are of no avail, unless a gracious hand shall apply them to us. We are thirsty, but too faint to crawl to the water-brook. When a soldier is wounded in battle it is of little use for him to know that there are those at the hospital who can bind up his wounds, and medicines there to ease all the pains which he now suffers: what he needs is to be carried thither, and to have the remedies applied. It is thus with our souls, and to meet this need there is one, even the Spirit of truth, who takes of the things of Jesus, and applies them to us. Think not that Christ hath placed his joys on heavenly shelves that we may climb up to them for ourselves, but he draws near, and sheds his peace abroad in our hearts. O Christian, if thou art tonight laboring under deep distresses, thy Father does not give thee promises and then leave thee to draw them up from the Word like buckets from a well, but the promises he has written in the Word he will write anew on your heart. He will manifest his love to you, and by his blessed Spirit, dispel your cares and troubles. Be it known unto thee, O mourner, that it is God's prerogative to wipe every tear from the eye of his people. The good Samaritan did not say, "Here is the wine, and here is the oil for you"; he actually poured in the oil and the wine.[1] So Jesus not only gives you the sweet wine of the promise, but holds the golden chalice to your lips, and pours the life-blood into your mouth. The poor, sick, way-worn pilgrim is not merely strengthened to walk, but he is borne on eagles' wings.[2] Glorious gospel! which provides everything for the helpless, which draws nigh to us when we cannot reach after it – brings us grace before we seek for grace! Here is as much glory in the giving as in the gift. Happy people who have the Holy Spirit to bring Jesus to them. (Spurgeon, p. Evening Oct 22)

Footnotes:
1. Luke 10:25-37.
2. Isaiah 40:31.

84

Reading: John 17

"I sanctify myself for them ..." John 17:19

Let thy morning thoughts, my soul, be directed to this sweet view of thy Savior. Behold thy Jesus presenting himself as the Surety of his people before God and the Father. Having now received the call and authority of God the Father, and being fitted with a body suited to the service of a Redeemer, here see him entering upon the vast work, and, in those blessed words, declaring the cause of it – *I sanctify myself*. Did Jesus mean that he made himself more holy for the purpose? No, surely; for that was impossible. But by Jesus' sanctifying himself, must be understood (as the Nazarite from the womb, consecrated, set apart, dedicated to the service to which the Father had called him) a voluntary offering – an holy unblemished sacrifice. And observe for whom: *for their sakes;* not for himself, for he needed it not. The priests under the law made their offerings, first for themselves, and then for the people.[1] But such an High-Priest became us, who is holy, harmless, undefiled, separate from sinners, and made higher than the heavens; and who needed not daily, as those high priests, so to offer. For the law maketh men high-priests which have infirmity; but the Son is consecrated for evermore.[2] My soul! pause over this view of thy Jesus; and when thou hast duly pondered it, go to the mercy-seat, under the Spirit's leadings and influences, and there, by faith, behold thy Jesus, in his vesture dipped in blood, there sanctified, and there appearing in the presence of God for thee. There plead the dedication of Jesus; for it is of the Father's own appointment. There tell thy God and Father (for it is the Father's glory when a poor sinner glorifies his dear Son in him) that He, that Holy One, whom the Father consecrated, and with an oath confirmed in his high-priestly office for ever, appeareth there for thee. Tell God that thy High-Priest's holiness and sacrifice was altogether holy, pure, without a spot; and both his Person, and his nature, and offering, clean as God's own righteous law. Tell, my soul, tell thy God and Father these sacred solemn truths. And while thou art thus coming to the mercy-seat, under the leadings of the Spirit, and wholly in the name and office-work of thy God and Savior, look unto Jesus, and call to mind those sweet words, for whose sake that Holy One sanctified himself; and then drop a petition more before thou comest from the heavenly court: beg, and pray, and wrestle, with the bountiful Lord, for, suited strength and grace, that as, for thy sake, among the other poor sinners of his redemption-love, Jesus sanctified himself, so thou mayest be able to be separated from everything but Jesus; and as thy happiness was Christ's end, so his glory may be thy first and greatest object. Yes, dearest Jesus! methinks I hear thee say, thou shalt be for me, and not for another: so will I be for thee. Oh! thou condescending, loving God! make me thine, that whether I live, I may live unto the Lord; or whether I die, I may die unto the Lord; so that living or dying I may be thine.[3] (Hawker, The Poor Man's Morning Portion, p. Mar 14)

Footnotes:
1. Leviticus 9:5-8.
2. Hebrews 6:20.
3. Romans 14:7-8.

85

Reading: Mark 15

"Pilate was surprised that he was already dead..." Mark 15:44

Precious Jesus! had the unjust judge but known thy soul-travail and agonies, instead of wondering at the speediness of thy death, all his astonishment would have been, that nature, so oppressed, and so suffering, could have held out so long; for what would have crushed in a moment all creation, as well angels as men, in sustaining the wrath of God, due to sin, Jesus endured on the cross for so many hours! In point of suffering, he wrought out a whole eternity due to sin on the cross; and in point of efficacy, he "forever perfected them that are sanctified." Jesus, therefore, accomplished more in that memorable day, than all the creatures of God could have done for ever. Wonderful were the works which God dispatched in creation; but the wonders of redemption far exceed them. The *six hours* which Jesus hung upon the cross wrought out a more stupendous display of almighty power and grace than the *six days* God was pleased to appoint to himself in making the world. But, indeed, Pilate need not, on another account, have marveled at the quickness of Christ's death, had this unjust judge but reflected on the previous sufferings of the Redeemer. They who have spent sweet hours in tracing Jesus's footsteps through the painful preludes to his death, and especially in the concluding scenes, have been able to mark many a sorrowful part which (besides the soul-agonies of Jesus in accomplishing redemption-work) bore hard upon his body also. My soul, if thou wert to trace back the solemn subject, thou wouldst find enough to excite thy astonishment that Jesus lived so long on the cross, rather than that he died not before. His agony evidently began *four days* before the Passover. The evangelist Luke tells us, that he spent the whole night in prayer, and the whole day in preaching, to the people in the temple.[1] Read also Matthew's account *four days* before his crucifixion, in the prospect of what was coming on.[2] And again, before a single assault was made upon him in the garden.[3] "My soul is exceeding sorrowful," said the dying Lamb, "even unto death." And the beloved apostle's relation is to the same amount, four days before his crucifixion: "Now is my soul troubled (said the holy Sufferer); and what shall I say? Father, save me from this hour! But for this cause came I unto this hour!"[4] And if to these agonies of soul, before the tremendous season of *Gethsemane* and *Golgotha* arrived, must be added the exercises of the Redeemer in body, all must have contributed to wear out and exhaust his strength, and hasten on the pains of death. When we call to mind how the Lamb of God was driven to and fro, hurried from one place to another, from Annas to Caiaphas, and from the judgment-hall to Calvary, we cannot be surprised at his fainting under the burden of his cross. Many a mile of weariness did he walk before nine of the clock in the morning of the day of his crucifixion: and many a bodily fainting must he have felt from the thorny crown, the soldier's scourging, and their buffetings and smitings with the palms of their hands. Unfeeling Pilate! thy marvellings will be now, and to all eternity, of another kind. As for thee, my soul, take thy stand at the foot of the cross, and do thou marvel whilst thou art looking up and beholding Jesus dying, that he who might have commanded twelve legions of angels to his rescue, should, in love to his Church and people, thus give "his soul an offering for sin," and die, "the just for the unjust, to bring us unto God!"[5] (Hawker, The Poor Man's Evening Portion, p. Apr 8)

Footnotes:
1. Luke 21:37-38.
2. Matthew 20:18-19.
3. Matthew 26:38.
4. John 12:27.
5. Isaiah 53:10; 1 Peter 3:18.

86

Reading: Matthew 27

"*Behold, the veil of the temple was rent in twain from the top to the bottom.*" Matthew 27:51 (AKJV)

No mean miracle was wrought in the rending of so strong and thick a veil; but it was not intended merely as a display of power – many lessons were herein taught us. *The old law of ordinances was put away,*[1] and like a worn-out vesture, rent and laid aside. When Jesus died, the sacrifices were all finished, because all fulfilled in him, and therefore the place of their presentation was marked with an evident token of decay. That rent also *revealed all the hidden things of the old dispensation*: the mercy-seat could now be seen, and the glory of God gleamed forth above it. By the death of our Lord Jesus we have a clear revelation of God, for he was "not as Moses, who put a veil over his face."[2] Life and immortality are now brought to light, and things which have been hidden since the foundation of the world are manifest in him. *The annual ceremony of atonement was thus abolished.* The atoning blood which was once every year sprinkled within the veil, was now offered once for all by the great High

Priest, and therefore the place of the symbolical rite was broken up. No blood of bullocks or of lambs is needed now, for Jesus has entered within the veil with his own blood. Hence *access to God is now permitted*, and is the privilege of every believer in Christ Jesus.[3] There is no small space laid open through which we may peer at the mercy-seat, but the rent reaches from the top to the bottom. We may come with boldness to the throne of the heavenly grace.[4] Shall we err if we say that the opening of the Holy of Holies in this marvelous manner by our Lord's expiring cry was *the type of the opening of the gates of paradise* to all the saints by virtue of the Passion? Our bleeding Lord hath the key of heaven; he openeth and no man shutteth; let us enter in with him into the heavenly places, and sit with him there till our common enemies shall be made his footstool.[5] (Spurgeon, p. Morning Apr 19)

Footnotes:
1. Colossians 2:14, referring to the law given to Moses.
2. 2 Corinthians 3:13.
3. Hebrews 10:12-19.
4. Hebrews 4:16.
5. Revelation 3:7; Ephesians 2:6; Hebrews 1:13; Psalm 110:1.

87

Reading: John 18

"Jesus said unto them, 'If ye seek me, let these go their way.'" John 18:8

Mark, my soul, the care which Jesus manifested even in his hour of trial, towards the sheep of his hand! The ruling passion is strong in death. He resigns himself to the enemy, but he interposes a word of power to set his disciples free. As to himself, like a sheep before her shearers he is dumb and opened not his mouth,[1] but for his disciples' sake he speaks with almighty energy. Herein is love, constant, self-forgetting, faithful love. But is there not far more here than is to be found upon the surface? Have we not the very soul and spirit of the atonement in these words? The Good Shepherd lays down his life for the sheep,[2] and pleads that they must therefore go free. The Surety is bound, and justice demands that those for whom he stands a substitute should go their way. In the midst of Egypt's bondage, that voice rings as a word of power, "Let these go their way." Out of slavery of sin and Satan the redeemed must come. In every cell of the dungeons of Despair, the sound is echoed, "Let these go their way," and forth come Despondency and Much-afraid. Satan hears the well-known voice, and lifts his foot from the neck of the fallen; and Death hears it, and the grave opens her gates to let the dead arise. Their way is one of progress, holiness, triumph, glory, and none shall dare to stay them in it. No lion shall be on their way, neither shall any ravenous beast go up thereon. "The hind of the morning"[3] has drawn the cruel hunters upon himself, and now the most timid roes and hinds of the field may graze at perfect peace among the lilies of his loves. The thunder-cloud has burst over the Cross of Calvary, and the pilgrims of Zion shall never be smitten by the bolts of vengeance. Come, my heart, rejoice in the immunity which thy Redeemer has secured thee, and bless his name all the day, and every day. (Spurgeon, p. Morning Mar 26)

Footnotes:
1. Acts 8:32; Mark 15:3; Mark 15:5.
2. John 10:11.
3. Poetic title given to Psalm 22.

88

Reading: John 19

"When Jesus had received the sour wine, he said, 'It is finished.'"
John 19:30

Perhaps these words formed the *sixth* cry of the Lord Jesus on the cross. The glorious close of all his sufferings was now arrived; and, full of these high ideas which occupied his holy mind, he cried out, "It is finished." What is finished? Redemption work is finished. All the long series of prophesies, visions, types, and the shadow of the good things to come, which pointed to Jesus, and redemption by him, were now finished in their accomplishment. The law was finished in its condemning power; and the gospel commenced its saving influence. Jesus, by that one sacrifice now offered, had forever perfected them that were sanctified.[1] The separation between Jew and Gentile was now finished, and done away forever. Jesus had now gathered together in one all the children of God which were scattered abroad. The iron reign of sin and Satan, of death and hell, were now broken in pieces by this Stone cut out of the mountain without hands; and life and immortality, pardon, mercy, and peace, were brought to light, and secured to the faithful, by this finished redemption of the Lord Jesus Christ. The peace, the love, the favor of God the Father, was now manifested, and that spiritual kingdom of the Lord Jesus, which shall have no end, was from this moment set up in the hearts and minds of his people. The sure descent of the Holy Spirit was now confirmed; and the Lord Jesus already, by anticipation, beheld his Israel of old, and his Gentile church, as well as Ethiopia and the multitude of the isles, stretching forth their hands unto God. With these and the like glorious prospects the mind of Jesus was filled; and having received the vinegar, as the last prophecy remaining then to be completed, he cried out, "It is finished." My soul! never let these precious, precious words of Jesus depart from thy mind. Do by them as Moses commanded Israel concerning the words he gave them; let them be in thy heart and in thy soul: bind them as a sign upon thine hand, and let them be as frontlets between thine eyes.[2] Tell thy God and Father what thy Jesus has told thee – "It is finished."[3] He hath finished redemption *for* thee; and He will finish redemption *in* thee. He hath destroyed death, hath satisfied and glorified the law, taken away the curse, made full restitution for sin, brought in an everlasting righteousness, and opened the glorious mansions of the blessed as the home and rest of all his people. Oh! my soul, let these dying words of thy Jesus be made by thee as an answer to all thy prayers, and begin that song to the Lamb, which, ere long thou wilt fully and loudly sing among the church above – Worthy is the Lamb that was slain; for thou wast slain, and has redeemed us to God by thy blood.[4] (Hawker, The Poor Man's Morning Portion, p. Apr 14)

Footnotes:
1. Hebrews 10:14.
2. Deuteronomy 6:8.
3. John 19:30.

4. Revelation 5:12.

89

Reading: Luke 23

"On him they laid the cross, that he might bear it after Jesus." Luke 23:26

We see in Simon's carrying the cross a picture of the work of the Church throughout all generations; she is the cross-bearer after Jesus. Mark then, Christian, Jesus does not suffer so as to exclude your suffering. He bears a cross, not that you may escape it, but that you may endure it. Christ exempts you from sin, but not from sorrow. Remember that, and expect to suffer.

But let us comfort ourselves with this thought, that in our case, as in Simon's, *it is not our cross, but Christ's cross which we carry.* When you are molested for your piety; when your religion brings the trial of cruel mockings upon you, then remember it is not your cross, it is Christ's cross; and how delightful is it to carry the cross of our Lord Jesus![1]

You carry the cross after him. You have blessed company; your path is marked with the footprints of your Lord. The mark of his blood-red shoulder is upon that heavy burden. 'Tis his cross, and he goes before you as a shepherd goes before his sheep. Take up your cross daily, and follow him.[2]

Do not forget, also, *that you bear this cross in partnership.* It is the opinion of some that Simon only carried one end of the cross, and not the whole of it. That is very possible; Christ may have carried the heavier part, against the transverse beam, and Simon may have borne the lighter end. Certainly, it is so with you; you do but carry the light end of the cross, Christ bore the heavier end.

And remember, *though Simon had to bear the cross for a very little while, it gave him lasting honor.* Even so the cross we carry is only for a little while at most, and then we shall receive the crown, the glory. Surely, we should love the cross, and, instead of shrinking from it, *count it very dear,* when it works out for us "a far more exceeding and eternal weight of glory."[3] (Spurgeon, p. Morning Apr 5)

Footnotes:
1. John 7:7; 1 Peter 3:13-17.
2. Luke 9:23.
3. 2 Corinthians 4:17.

90

Reading: Mark 16

"He that believeth and is baptized shall be saved." Mark 16:16

Mr. MacDonald asked the inhabitants of the island of St. Kilda how a man must be saved. An old man replied, "We shall be saved if we repent, and forsake our sins, and turn to God." "Yes," said a middle-aged female, "and with a true heart too." "Aye," rejoined a third, "and with prayer"; and, added a fourth, "It must be the prayer of the heart." "And we must be diligent too," said a fifth, "in keeping the commandments." Thus, each having contributed his mite, feeling that a very decent creed had been made up, they all looked and listened for the preacher's approbation, but they had aroused his deepest pity. The carnal mind always maps out for itself a way in which self can work and become great, but the Lord's way is quite the reverse. Believing and being baptized are no matters of merit to be gloried in – they are so simple that boasting is excluded, and free grace bears the palm. It may be that the reader is unsaved – what is the reason? Do you think the way of salvation as laid down in the text to be dubious? How can that be when God has pledged his own word for its certainty? Do you think it too easy? Why, then, do you not attend to it? Its ease leaves those without excuse who neglect it. To believe is simply to trust, to depend, to rely upon Christ Jesus. To be baptized is to submit to the ordinance which our Lord fulfilled at Jordan, to which the converted ones submitted at Pentecost, to which the jailer yielded obedience the very night of his conversion. The outward sign saves not, but it sets forth to us our death, burial, and resurrection with Jesus, and, like the Lord's Supper, is not to be neglected. Reader, do you believe in Jesus? Then, dear friend, dismiss your fears, you shall be saved. Are you still an unbeliever, then remember there is but one door, and if you will not enter by it you will perish in your sins.[1] (Spurgeon, p. Evening Oct 5)

Footnote:
1. John 10:9.

91

Reading: Matthew 28

"Jesus came near and said to them, "All authority has been given to me in heaven and on earth."" Matthew 28:18

Hail then, thou Sovereign Lord of all! I have lately been following thee in sweet and solemn meditation through the seasons of thy humiliation; now let me behold thee on thy throne. And here I am called upon to contemplate my Lord and my God as possessing universal dominion. Ponder, my soul, the vast extent. Thy Jesus, as God, as one with the Father, possesseth in common with him all power from everlasting. This is his, as God, essentially so; not given to him, for by nature it is his, being "one with the Father, over all God blessed forever. Amen,"[1] said Paul, so let it be, so shall it be. And so say I, and so saith all the church: Amen, Amen. But what thy Jesus saith here, in these blessed words, is of a power *given* to him: and that is a power as the Head of his church and people. And although had he not been God, one with the Father, he never could have been suited for the exercise of this power; (for unless he had been the mighty God, how should he have been the mighty Redeemer?) yet being God, and both God and man, it is precious to consider the power that is given to the Lord Jesus as Jesus, the Head over all things to the church, which is his body, the fulness of Him that filleth all in all. Here then, my soul, let thy thoughts take wing this morning. Behold thy Jesus the Head over all principality and power. See him, by virtue of his Almighty Godhead, exercising and giving energy to the fulness of his power as Mediator; and in this view conceive if it be possible, to what an extent thy Jesus is unceasingly exercising his power for the everlasting benefit of his church and people. All power in heaven: not only among the highest order of created being, angels and archangels, but a power with God the Father to prevail for the eternal salvation of all his redeemed. He left it as a record how he exercised this power when he said before his departure, Father, I will that they whom thou hast given me, be with me where I am, to behold my glory."[2] And he hath power to send the Holy Spirit to all his people. He said himself, before he went away, "If I go not away, the Comforter will not come; but if I depart, I will send him unto you."[3] Here then, my soul, here let thy thoughts be directed, to meditate upon the fulness and extensiveness of that power which thy Jesus possesseth in heaven. Well may it be said that he hath the keys of heaven, when he hath all power with the Father and with the Spirit. And well may it be said that he hath the keys of hell also, when all things in heaven and earth, and under the earth, are subject to his command. And hath he not power then, my soul, suited to answer every want of thine, and of all his church and people? Hath he not power over all flesh, to give eternal life to as many as the Father hath given him? Wilt thou complain, shall the church complain, of any want, while Jesus is upon the throne? Art thou poor, is the church poor, weak, helpless, needy, guilty, polluted, oppressed, exercised? What of all these, and ten thousand other situations, while Jesus lives, and hath all power? Nay, is it not so much the better that the people of Jesus are what they are, that they may be the better suited for his glory, and that their wants may give occasion for the supplies of his grace? Hail! thou Almighty Sovereign, now methinks I would be always poor, always needy, always feeling my nothingness, that all these may constrain me to come to thee: so that every day's necessities may afford a fresh occasion to crown thee Lord of all in a day of grace until I come to crown thee, with the whole church, the everlasting Lord of all in heaven, to the glory of God the Father. Amen. (Hawker, The Poor Man's Morning Portion, p. May 30)

Footnotes:
1. Romans 9:5; John 17:22.
2. John 17:24.
3. John 16:7.

92

Reading: John 20

"... he showed them his hands and his side ..." John 20:20

My Lord and my God! I would say, while thou openest to me such a view, and while I would look into and read thine heart in it. And what was such a display designed for, dearest Lord? I think thou hast taught me to discover. Was it not as if Jesus had said, "See here the marks of your sure redemption. From hence issued the blood that hath cleansed you from all sin. And this blood hath a voice. It is *speaking* blood, which speaketh better things than that of Abel.[1] For *his* blood cried for vengeance,[2] *mine* for pardon. It speaketh *for* thee *to* my Father of his covenant promises. And it speaketh *to* thee *from* my Father of thy sure acceptance in my salvation." – Neither was this all. For surely, dearest Jesus, when thou showedst thine hands and thy side, it was also as if thou hadst said, "See here an opening to my heart. Here put in all you wish to tell my Father, and I will bear it to him with all my warmest affections. And let all my disciples, in every age of my Church, do this. I will be the bearer of all their suits. And sure they may be, both of my love and of my success for them; for I will carry all that concerns them in this opening to my heart." Precious Lord! cause me often to view with the eye of faith this gracious interview of thine with thy disciples. And as in the evening of the day, the disciples were thus favored with thy presence, and so rich a manifestation of thy love, so, Lord, make me to realize the scene afresh, and very often in the silence of the night may my soul be going forth in the full enjoyment of this spiritual blessing! Yea, Jesus! let me behold thine hands and thy side, and learn day by day to put therein all I would tell my God and Father of thy great salvation, and my firm reliance upon it; until from a life of faith I come to enter upon a life of absolute enjoyment, and behold thee still as the Lamb that hath been slain for the redemption of thy people, in the midst of the throne, leading the church to living fountains of waters, where all tears are wiped away from all eyes.[3] (Hawker, The Poor Man's Evening Portion, p. Jan 3)

Footnotes:
1. Hebrews 12:24.
2. Genesis 4:8-10.
3. Revelation 7:17.

93

Reading: John 21

"A second time he asked him, "Simon, son of John, do you love me?" "Yes, Lord," he said to him, "you know that I love you." John 21:16

"God is love,"[1] and the expression of that love is the sending His own Son into the world, to achieve what the law, in its weakness, could not do. Was ever love like this? "God so loved."[2] And was Jesus willing to engage in the embassy? Did He voluntarily clothe Himself in our rags, stoop to our poverty, consent to be arrested and thrown into prison for us? Was He made a curse that He might deliver us from the curse?[3] Did judgment pass upon Him, that we might be saved from the wrath to come?[4] Oh here is infinite, boundless love! Then let Him have in return our love; it is the least that He can ask, or we can make. Let it be a hearty, cordial, obedient, increasing love. Alas! It is but a drop, when it should be an ocean. It is but a faint spark, when it should be a vehement flame.

How should our best affection flow out toward Him who assumed, and stills wears, our nature! What an attractive, winning object is the Incarnate God, the God-man Mediator! Fairer than the children of men, the chief among ten thousand, the altogether lovely, He is the wonder and admiration, the beloved and the song, of all heaven. Why should He not be equally so of all earth? Did the Son of God take up our rude and suffering nature, and shall we be both to take up His lowly and despised cross, and follow hard after Him? Forbid it, Lord! Forbid it, you precious Savior! What humiliation, what abasement, can be too much for us, the sinful sons of men, when You, the sinless Son of God, did so abase and humble Yourself! Let Your love constrain us to stand firm to You, to Your truth, and to Your cause, when the world despises, when friends forsake, when relatives look cold, and all seem to leave and forsake us. And as You did condescend to be made in the likeness of our human and sinful nature,[5] oh conform us to the likeness of Your Divine and holy nature. As You were a partaker with us, make us partakers with You. As You were made like unto us, in what was proper to man, make us like You, in what is proper to God. And as You did come down to our sinful and dim earth; lift us to Your pure and bright heaven!

What a privilege is nearness to Christ! Yet, dear and precious as it is, how sadly is it overlooked! We may trace this, in some degree, to the believer's oversight of his oneness with Christ. Yet to forget this truth is to forget that He lives. As the branch has one life with the vine, the graft one life with the tree, so he that is united to Christ, and grafted into Christ, has one life with Christ. Go where he may, he is one with Christ. Be his circumstances what they may, he is one with Christ. And as he is in Christ, so Christ is in him. And if Christ be in him, dwelling in him, living in him, walking in him, so also is Christ in every event, and incident, and circumstance of his history. He cannot look upon the darkest cloud that overhangs his path, but he may say, "Christ is in my cloud; Christ is in my sorrow; Christ is in my conflict; Christ is in my need; Christ is all to me, and Christ is in all with me." (Winslow, Evening Thoughts, p. Jun 17)

Footnotes:
1. 1 John 4:8.
2. John 3:16.
3. Galatians 3:13.
4. Romans 5:9.
5. Romans 8:3.

94

Reading: Luke 24

"*He expounded unto them in all the Scriptures the things concerning himself.*" Luke 24:27

The two disciples on the road to Emmaus had a most profitable journey. Their companion and teacher was *the best of tutors*; the interpreter one of a thousand, in whom are hid all the treasures of wisdom and knowledge.[1] The Lord Jesus condescended to become a preacher of the gospel, and he was not ashamed to exercise his calling before an audience of two persons, neither does he now refuse to become the teacher of even one. Let us court the company of so excellent an Instructor, for till he is made unto us wisdom we shall never be wise unto salvation.

This unrivalled tutor used as his class-book *the best of books*. Although able to reveal fresh truth, he preferred to expound the old. He knew by his omniscience what was the most instructive way of teaching, and by turning at once to Moses and the prophets, he showed us that the surest road to wisdom is not speculation, reasoning, or reading human books, but meditation upon the Word of God. The readiest way to be spiritually rich in heavenly knowledge is to dig in this mine of diamonds, to gather pearls from this heavenly sea. When Jesus himself sought to enrich others, he wrought in the quarry of Holy Scripture.

The favored pair were led to consider *the best of subjects*, for Jesus spake of Jesus, and expounded the things concerning himself. Here the diamond cut the diamond, and what could be more admirable? The Master of the House unlocked his own doors, conducted the guests to his table, and placed his own dainties upon it. He who hid the treasure in the field himself guided the searchers to it. Our Lord would naturally discourse upon the sweetest of topics, and he could find none sweeter than his own person and work: with an eye to these we should always search the Word. O for grace to study the Bible with Jesus as both our teacher and our lesson! (Spurgeon, p. Evening Jan 18)

Footnote:
1. Colossians 2:3.

Works Cited

2017. *Christian Standard Bible.* Nashville, TN: Holman Bible Publisher.

Hawker, Robert. 1815. *Poor Man's New Testament Commentary: Matthew-John.* Vol. 1. London: Sherwood, Neely and Jones.

—. 1845. *The Poor Man's Evening Portion.* A New Edition. Philadelphia: Thomas Wardle.

—. 1845. *The Poor Man's Morning Portion.* Pittsburg: Robert Carter.

Spurgeon, C. H. 1896. *Morning and Evening: Daily readings.* London: Passmore & Alabaster.

Winslow, Octavius. 1856. *Evening Thoughts.* Leamington, England.

—. 1856. *Morning Thoughts.* Leamington, England.

Robert Hawker (1753–1827):

Robert Hawker, a Royal Marine assistant surgeon, Anglican priest, and author, was born 1753 in Exeter, England. He was married aged 19 to Anna Rains, and they had eight children altogether. He was ordained as a minister in 1779. It was in the pulpit that "the Doctor" was best known and loved. Thousands flocked to hear the "Star of the West" preach when he was in London. An Evangelical, he preached the Bible and proclaimed the love of God. (Wikipedia: Robert Hawker 2020)

Charles H. Spurgeon (1834-1892):

Charles Haddon Spurgeon, an English Particular Baptist preacher and author, was born on 19 June 1834 in Kelvedon, Essex, England. He married Susannah Thompson in 1856 and had twin boys. Spurgeon remains highly influential among Christians of various denominations, among whom he is known as the "Prince of Preachers." (Wikipedia: Charles Spurgeon 2020)

Octavius Winslow (1808-1878):

Octavius Winslow, a pastor and author, was born on 1 August 1808 in Pentonville, a village near London. In 1834 he married Hannah Ann Ring and had ten children with her. He pastored churches in both America and England, spending most of his life in England. He was also known as "The Pilgrim's Companion," and was a prominent 19th-century evangelical preacher in England and America. (Wikipedia: Octavius Winslow 2020)

C.M.H. Koenig Books

Bite-sized,
chronological Scripture readings &
accompanying devotionals —
great for those with a busy schedule.

www.cmhkoenigbooks.net

AVAILABLE NOW

Online Bookstores

www.ingramcontent.com/pod-product-compliance
Lightning Source LLC
Chambersburg PA
CBHW071430070526
44578CB00001B/61